BEING UNEQUAL

BEING UNEQUAL

How Identity Helps Make and Break Power and Privilege

Peter L. Callero

ROWMAN & LITTLEFIELD
Lanham • Boulder • New York • London

Published by Rowman & Littlefield
A wholly owned subsidiary of
The Rowman & Littlefield Publishing Group, Inc.
4501 Forbes Boulevard, Suite 200, Lanham, Maryland 20706
https://rowman.com

Unit A, Whitacre Mews, 26-34 Stannary Street, London SE11 4AB,
United Kingdom

British Library Cataloguing in Publication Information Available

Library of Congress Cataloging-in-Publication Data
Names: Callero, Peter L., author.
Title: Being unequal : how identity helps make and break power and privilege /
    Peter Callero.
Description: Lanham : Rowman & Littlefield, [2017] | Includes bibliographical
    references and index.
Identifiers: LCCN 2017015829 (print) | LCCN 2017023469 (ebook) | ISBN
    9781538100578 (electronic) | ISBN 9781538100554 (cloth : alk. paper) |
    ISBN 9781538100561 (pbk. : alk. paper)
Subjects: LCSH: Equality. | Social stratification. | Group identity. | Identity
    (Psychology)
Classification: LCC HM821 (ebook) | LCC HM821 .C35 2017 (print) | DDC
    305.5/12—dc23
LC record available at https://lccn.loc.gov/2017015829

For Roman Giovanni Callero, Lucia Antonia Callero,
and Mia Isabella Callero.
With greater empathy, solidarity, and political action,
may your world be more equal, just, and fair.

CONTENTS

ACKNOWLEDGMENTS

The idea for this book began in 2013 when I was invited to contribute a short chapter to the *Handbook of the Social Psychology of Inequality*. In conducting my research, I was fascinated to discover that the literature on identity and inequality was more wide-ranging, theoretically diverse, multidisciplinary, and intellectually vibrant than I had assumed. I also found that this body of knowledge was rather disparate and disconnected, and contained conceptual definitions that were often vague and sometimes contradictory. Organizing and integrating this branch of sociology proved to be both challenging and intellectually rewarding.

Coincidentally, at about the same time that I was conducting my research on identity and inequality, a number of sensational news stories focused the public's attention on identity and the legitimacy of specific identity claims. Bruce Jenner, the gold medal–winning Olympian and patriarch of television's celebrated Kardashians, announced his decision to transition from male to female. Rachel Dolezal, the president of the NAACP in Spokane, Washington, was "outed" as a white person with darkened skin and unnaturally curly hair. And Manti Te'o, the star linebacker on Notre Dame's football team, received national sympathy when he shared a heart-wrenching story of his online girlfriend, who was dying of cancer, only to be publicly humiliated when it was revealed he had been the victim of an elaborate hoax. It turned out that his "girlfriend" did not actually exist.

These and other incidents led a *New York Times* commentator to proclaim that 2015 was "The Year We Obsessed over Identity," and for many of the same reasons, *Time* magazine pronounced *identity* as the word of the year for 2015. It was clear to me that the popular news media and the general public were beginning to accept something sociologists have known for a very long time: Identity is *socially constructed*. Gender and race are not exclusively defined by biology, and the line separating "real" and "fake" identities is often fuzzy and crooked. But beyond this new fascination with the plasticity of identity, these sensational news stories also raised serious questions about power, social inequality, and the politics of identity. On these matters there is much debate, considerable confusion, and very little knowledge of sociological research. Identity may be a newfound concern, but our public discourse on the matter is not well informed by theory and research in the social sciences. My decision to write *Being Unequal* was motivated by a commitment to public sociology and a belief that science, knowledge, and truth may move us closer to equality, peace, and justice.

With one important difference, this book is essentially an expansion of the chapter that was eventually published in the *Handbook of the Social Psychology of Inequality*. The primary difference between the *Handbook* chapter and this book is the intended audience. The analytical framework that structured the *Handbook* chapter remains the same, but this book's elaboration adds more examples from research, avoids technical jargon as much as possible, and includes numerous personal stories with the hope of creating a more inviting narrative. My goal all along has been to translate the academic language of professional sociologists into a style and structure that are more attractive to a general audience, especially students.

Several people have contributed to the completion of this project. I want to first thank Jane McLeod of Indiana University, Ed Lawler at the University of Iowa, and Michael Schwalbe at North Carolina State University. These three sociologists served as editors of the *Handbook of the Social Psychology of Inequality*, and it was their invitation that indirectly nudged this book into existence. Jane and Mike were especially supportive of my work on the *Handbook* chapter. They read several early drafts, identified gaps in my research, and offered helpful suggestions for improving the clarity of my writing. Both Mike and Jane are also leading scholars in the social psychology of inequality, and their research (in different ways) has significantly advanced our understanding of how inequality is created, how it is reproduced, and how it harms our health and dignity.

Dean Braa and Maureen Dolan, my colleagues in the sociology department at Western Oregon University, have both had an enormous impact on my thinking, especially on matters of identity, inequality, and social change. Dean read and commented on an early draft of the book manuscript. His influence is most evident in the threads of *critical realism* that are woven into the pages of this book. As a philosophy of science, critical realism reminds us that good theory and good research require a solid philosophical grounding in the ontology of agency, structure, culture, and truth.

Scott Harris at St. Louis University also provided a careful and close reading of the entire manuscript. His comments and suggested changes have made the book more academically sound, more sensitive to diverse interpretations and, at the same time, better organized and more useful for students.

Other colleagues, friends, and relatives who have indirectly contributed to my understanding of inequality and identity through discussion, debate, and example also deserve credit. This list includes Jane Piliavin (University of Wisconsin–Madison), Judy Howard (University of Washington), Rick Zimmerman (University of Missouri–St. Louis), and Tri van Nguyen (La Salle University). Vern Callero Sr. also read and commented on an early draft, and, although they were not formal readers, the other members of the big, diverse, and unequal Callero/DeFuria family had a hand in this book in subtle but profound ways.

At Rowman & Littlefield, both Sarah Stanton and Carli Hansen played valuable roles in the editing and production process. I am grateful for their professionalism, patience, and support.

Finally, a special thank-you to Kathleen DeFuria Callero, who works daily with families who have been trapped in the net of poverty and inequality. Her empathy and commitment to human dignity is a source of inspiration, motivation, and pride.

INTRODUCTION

On the morning of September 17, 2011, an estimated two thousand demonstrators gathered in Lower Manhattan in front of the New York Stock Exchange to express their anger and frustration with "corporate rule" and the unjust power of the wealthiest "one percent." The objective of the protest: Occupy Wall Street and inspire a social movement to advance the economic interests of the 99 percent. Most observers assumed that the rally would end in a matter of hours, but when police officers cordoned off the financial district, the activists moved three blocks north to a small plaza known as Zuccotti Park. By nightfall, hundreds of citizens had set up tents, established food pantries, and formed a general assembly—they were in for the long haul.

Initial media coverage of the encampment was limited, but as the occupation continued, public demonstrations grew in size and strength—and the world began to take notice. Within weeks, similar camps were being formed in hundreds of small and large towns throughout the United States. Then on October 15, four weeks after the first protesters gathered on Wall Street, massive demonstrations of solidarity occurred in cities across the globe, including London, Rome, Madrid, Hong Kong, Seoul, Santiago, Porto Alegre, Melbourne, and Istanbul. What began as a loosely knit gathering of social activists had exploded into a global movement for economic justice.

Three years after the Occupy Movement focused the world's attention on the concentration of wealth and power, an English language translation of a six-hundred-page monograph written by a French economist was published in the United States. To the surprise of many, Thomas Piketty's book, *Capital in the Twenty-First Century*, reached number one on the *New York Times* nonfiction best seller list, eventually became the top seller on Amazon.com, and is now the highest-selling book in the history of its publisher.

Capital in the Twenty-First Century offers a careful and systematic examination of the accumulation and distribution of wealth over the last century. It is a relatively dense academic tome filled with mathematical analyses of capital/income ratios, purchasing power, growth rates, tax rates, inheritance flows, and income inequality—not the content of your typical best seller. But with painstaking precision, Piketty offers compelling evidence that the hyperconcentration of wealth and income in the bank accounts and investment portfolios of a very small minority of the population is the normal and expected outcome of a capitalist economy. In short, the rich get richer because wealth grows faster than wages, and fortunes are passed on from one generation to the next. In Piketty's own words, a market economy based on private property contains powerful forces that "are potentially threatening to democratic societies and to the values of social justice on which they are based."[1]

In different ways, the unanticipated public response to both the Occupy protesters and Piketty's book reveals a mounting concern with the problem of inequality. Whereas the Occupy Movement revealed the heart and passion of a people disturbed by the everyday injustices of poverty and diminishing opportunity, Piketty's laborious research presents the objective evidence that economic inequality is indeed real, historically persistent, and growing. In their own way, the Occupy demonstrations gave voice to an oppressed class of people simmering with frustration, while the publication of *Capital in the Twenty-First Century* provided compelling economic data validating their anger. Clearly, both events struck a chord for many millions of people around the world.

This book is also a social scientific examination of inequality. But unlike Piketty's macroeconomic analysis of historical data, I concentrate on the micro-sociological implications of identity, and focus my analysis on the lived experience of actual persons. In this sense, you could say that my perspective falls somewhere between the personal commitment of the Occupy protesters and the dispassionate analysis of an economic investigation. How do individuals experience inequality? What is the

impact of inequality on the self? What social processes work to reproduce and sustain inequality at the level of interaction? And what social
practices are used to resist and reform inequality? These are some of
the questions that I will address.

In simplest terms, an identity can be understood as a social classifi-
cation or label that we use to categorize and "identify" each other (and
ourselves) as we make our way through life. Some identity categories
refer to a person's physical characteristics (tall, black, female), group
memberships (Catholic, Teamster, Democrat), occupation(s) (dish-
washer, lawyer, truck driver), or family roles (mother, cousin, daughter). Others define roles in organizations (captain, treasurer, volunteer)
or particular social achievements (college graduate, award winner, retired). Some speak to qualities of our character (optimist, dishonest,
smart), our sexual preferences (gay, straight, bisexual), or our past behavior (ex-convict, former president, war veteran). And as these examples suggest, some identity categories cast a wide net and may be deeply
meaningful, while others are rather narrow and relatively inconsequential.

The nature of identity has been intensely investigated and hotly
debated within multiple academic disciplines for almost two thousand
years. Some of these arguments are little more than exercises in seman-
tics, but there are also disputes over the basic assumptions of personhood, individuality, and the nature of the self.[2] Early philosophers
struggled with questions concerning the relationship of identity to the
soul, morality, and the continuity of the body, and modern psychology
has examined identity in terms of brain function, the cognitive processing of information, and the development of personality.[3] While insights
from this large and diverse body of scholarship are valuable, understanding the link between identity and inequality demands a sociological perspective.

From a sociological point of view, all identities emerge from social
relationships, are sustained by social relationships, and are altered by
changes in social relationships.[4] This does not mean, however, that
identity is completely determined by social forces. Individuality, creativity, and agency are also a part of identity, and sociologists recognize
that there is both a personal or subjective dimension of identity (who I
am, what I feel and think about myself) and a socially shared or inter-
subjective side (who another is, what the community thinks and feels

about that other person). This is an important point, for it is the inter-subjectivity of identities that serves as a bridge linking the individual self and the larger social structures, institutions, and cultural practices that define society.

When it comes to inequality, some identity categories matter more than others. Some play a sustained and critical role in the making and breaking of power and privilege. Here, gender, race, and class are key, but age, physical ability, and sexual orientation are also especially salient. When we experience inequality based on an identity category, it is because a dominant class of people has enough power and control to establish and reinforce a negative or devalued interpretation of the identity. When social movements and protest organizations are successful in establishing greater equality, it is because they have wrestled power, control, and resources away from a dominant group and, in the process, redefined the meaning of an oppressed identity.

Most social scientists will argue that identity categories are merely social constructions—human inventions—that are particular to a specific culture and time. And it is true that there is nothing inherently natural, universal, or permanent about specific identity labels. It is also true that the same identity category might have very different meanings or interpretations for different groups of people. But as I will show in the chapters that follow, identity categories and identity processes are, nevertheless, critical elements in the making and breaking of inequality. Identities may be cultural inventions, but they are rooted in tangible social relationships that have very real consequences for actual human persons. The relative value and power attached to categories of race, ethnicity, gender, and class, for example, can have an enormous impact on the direction of a person's life by controlling economic opportunities and influencing both physical and mental health. And as I will show later, the very same identity categories are also employed in the structuring of powerful economic, political, and cultural institutions that help manufacture inequality.

At its core, inequality is about the unequal distribution of material resources. And in the modern global economy, the procedures for distributing valued material resources are largely ordered by the structures of capitalism and the rules of inherited wealth. Yet we must also recognize that inequality is not exclusively economic. Power and privilege may flow from the concentration of income and wealth, but structures of inequality are also designed, decorated, and reinforced with cultural traditions, linguistic tropes, political interpretations, and shared understandings of identity.

All social institutions emerge from face-to-face interactions, and our most significant interactions demand the recognition and negotiation of identity categories. Economic institutions are no exception. Identities matter because they are part of a process whereby everyday interactions and relationships are converted into

1. patterns of structural inequality,
2. systems that legitimate and justify inequality, and
3. collective actions organized to resist and oppose domination and exploitation.

The social forces that produce and sustain inequality are obviously complex, and it would be a mistake to assume that inequality can be either reduced to the psychology of the individual or explained away as simply the rational operation of economic laws. Identity-related processes are only one part of an intricate system that also includes the legacy of historical events; formal and informal rules; institutionalized relations of power, control, and domination; and the dynamics of face-to-face interaction. In the following section I provide a short illustration of this larger sociological context with a rather innocuous personal experience from my childhood.

BASIC ELEMENTS OF INEQUALITY

Most of us have recollections from our childhood that remain vivid for one reason or another. Very often these long-term memories are the result of a traumatic event, an experience of anxiety, or a moment of joy, such as the death of a family member, the first day of school, or the birth of a sibling. But sometimes there are little snippets of life that we recall with great clarity for reasons that aren't always obvious. For me, one such moment occurred when I was six years old.

It was the summer of 1961 and I was sitting on the front-porch steps of our family home. We lived in the Capitol Hill district of Seattle, not far from the city's downtown core. This is a neighborhood known for its magnificent Victorian-era mansions and majestic views, but the houses on my block were mostly unpretentious, tightly packed, two-story homes, with a tiny patch of lawn in the front and a common alley in the back. At the time, it seemed as if all our neighbors were just like me— white, middle- and working-class families who sent their children to the Catholic school two blocks away. Everyone looked and sounded familiar to me. For this reason, I was surprised, that warm summer afternoon, to see a stranger walking down the sidewalk in front of our house. I remember leaping from the front stoop and running into our kitchen to find my mother. "Mom! Mom! Guess what I just saw!" My screeching must have alarmed her because I remember that she turned with a worried look on her face. "What? What is it?" she said. I paused for dramatic effect and exclaimed, "I just saw a Negro man on our sidewalk!"

This was not the first time I had seen a person of color. In fact, there was an entire black community just five blocks east of our street. I was used to seeing African Americans on the buses, in the city parks, and shopping in the local stores. But I had never seen a person of color on our street. I was both bewildered and amused. There was nothing unusual about the man himself. As I recall, he was young, of average height and weight, and dressed in a conventional style—nothing out of the norm. Still, the fact that this man was on our sidewalk looked outlandish and even comical. In my mind it was the equivalent of wearing a bathing suit to church or eating spaghetti without a fork. I thought to myself, "This is a huge story, and others will surely be impressed with my amazing discovery." But to my great disappointment, my mother's reaction was muted and strangely subdued. I expected her to be equally shocked. I wanted her to be stunned the same way that I was. But her eyes didn't widen, she didn't bolt outside to catch a glimpse for herself, and she didn't even giggle! She simply said, "Oh . . . well, that's OK," before returning to her household chores.

I remember feeling confused and perplexed. How can this be OK? If it's not "OK" to wear a bathing suit to Sunday mass, and if it's not "OK" to eat pasta with your hands, how could it be "OK" for a black man to walk down our sidewalk? In my juvenile mind, these were equivalent rules of behavior.

My family was not racist in any obvious way. I learned early on that the *n* word was wrong and should never be used, and I was taught in school that all people are equal in God's eyes and deserve to be valued and respected. Yet somehow, by the age of six, I was already aware of the rules governing racial segregation. I was not a special child in any sense of the term. There is no evidence that I was intellectually precocious, and I have no reason to believe that I was uniquely sensitive to issues of race. I was simply an average first grader who noticed a rather obvious pattern in my neighborhood: People with dark-colored skin lived east of Twenty-Third Avenue, and people with light-colored skin lived on the west side. In my mind this was part of the natural order of things, like short hair for boys and long hair for girls. It did not require explanation or justification; that's just the way it was.

With historical perspective, I can see now that this was my introduction to the complex reality of inequality. I did not associate any value—either positive or negative—with skin color. I was oblivious to the poison of prejudice and the humiliation of racial exclusion, and I knew nothing about the legacy of slavery or the gap of education, income, and wealth that separated whites and blacks. All I knew was what I saw: Blacks lived in one place and whites lived in another. When this blatant sorting of people and places was violated, it stood out like a kitten in a litter of puppies. I expected an all-white street because that was all I had ever experienced.

My mother may have said racial integration was "OK," but her view was not dominant. In fact, at that time, interracial marriage was still against the law in eighteen states, and segregation by race was still mostly legal across the country. More than fifty years have passed since that summer day in 1961 when a young black man disrupted my understanding of the social order, and over the past five decades our society has witnessed some enormous advances toward racial equality, including the election of an African American president. But when I recently returned to my old childhood neighborhood I noticed that Twenty-Third Avenue still serves as a geographic barrier between white families and families of color.[5] The segregation may not be as stark or as blatant, but there is no doubt that it still exists.

I share this childhood memory because it can serve as an introduction to five basic elements that are essential to understanding the making and breaking of inequality in our everyday lives. I will refer to these as

1. sociological legacy,
2. reproduction and resistance,
3. power,
4. rules, and
5. identity.

I will briefly review each of these ideas below and show how they are useful in understanding my youthful experience with racial segregation. Throughout the rest of this book I will return to these five themes as I explore the relationship between self and inequality in more depth. But before proceeding, I need to emphasize an important analytical caveat. When examining the experience of inequality in our everyday lives, one's focus naturally turns to the dynamic social processes and mechanisms that operate at the level of interaction. But this attention to the micro-sociology of communication should not lead us to the conclusion that inequality can be reduced to the circumstances of situations, the outcome of face-to-face conversations, or individual biases, preferences, and attitudes. Inequality is not that simple. We must keep in mind at all times that the macro-sociological forces associated with political and economic institutions, complex organizations, and cultural traditions are always and everywhere in the background. Inequality is layered in ways that are at times visible and are often unseen. This is best illustrated in the social circumstances we inherit from generations that come before us—in other words, our sociological legacy.

Sociological Legacy

For most of human history, material resources necessary for survival and comfort have been scarce or meager for some individuals while abundant for and hoarded by others. As a consequence, hunger, disease, poverty, fear, slavery, and servitude have always existed alongside health, happiness, freedom, dominance, and abundance. There are exceptions, of course, and there was a time in very early human history when relative equality may have existed, but in general terms, inequality has been the rule for most every human society over the past ten thousand years. This means that the unequal distribution of wealth, power, privilege, and social status that we witness today was firmly in place before any of us was born.

The racial segregation that I observed in my neighborhood as a six-year-old was well established prior to my birth. I had no more hand in building the policies and practices of segregation that characterized Seattle in 1961 than I did in establishing the African slave trade of 1661. In fact, racial segregation in Seattle not only preceded my birth, but it also preceded my parents' birth and the birth of every other person in my neighborhood. For this reason, segregation, and inequality more generally, can seem like an independent structure, or machine, that was constructed by our predecessors in the past but continues to operate on its own in the present. Like a runaway truck barreling downhill without a driver, inequality can feel like it is outside of our control. And as we will see in the pages that follow, the actions of prior generations are indeed a powerful force. No matter what our station in life, wealthy or poor, privileged or disrespected, a history of inequality forms the foundation of our personal life experience. If we are born into a poor family, our economic future will be constrained. If we are born female or a member of a racial minority, we will have fewer opportunities. And if we are lucky enough to be born into a family and neighborhood characterized by expensive homes, safe streets, and good schools, our economic future will be brighter, our bodies will be healthier, and life will be more pleasant.

But history is not destiny. The legacy of inequality may very well establish the context of our social life, but it does not determine all outcomes. The momentum of historical inequality can be overwhelming, but it does not have a life of its own, and it cannot persist without the assistance of contemporary actors. In other words, if the historical legacy of inequality continues to shape life outcomes, it is because it is being reproduced by successive generations.

Reproduction and Resistance

The historical precedence and persistence of inequality is difficult to explain if we think only in terms of isolated individuals making choices and acting on their own. It took the cooperative effort of many people to establish the slave trade, build a slave economy, and develop racially segregated institutions, and if the unequal distribution of resources based on race is to be maintained, it too requires the cooperation and joint activity of many people. The past may be prologue, but the prologue cannot write itself. In this way, the structure of inequality is less like a machine or runaway truck, and more like a language.

The English language, for example, has a recognizable structure defined by its vocabulary and rules of grammar, and no single person is responsible for its invention or its continuation. English as a language existed before all of us were born, and it will most certainly continue to exist after our death. But at the same time, the English language itself would disappear without a community of English language speakers. If nobody is around to speak or write the language, and nobody is around to hear or read the language, then the language cannot be reproduced. A language is not sustained in a dictionary or a book of grammar; it is kept alive by a community of language users. No one has to intentionally reproduce a language, but all users of a language are contributing to its reproduction.

In the chapters that follow we will see that the manner in which inequality is reproduced involves a wide range of related social processes. In the case of racial segregation, there are blatant policies of exclusion, such as a legislative body establishing separate schools for whites and blacks, or real estate developers and homeowners who cooperate to keep blacks out of a neighborhood. But at the same time, individuals engaged in face-to-face interaction also help reproduce racial segregation in subtler ways that typically go unnoticed. For example, in a very small way, I was already contributing to the structure of racial inequality in Seattle at the age of six. By calling attention to the "deviant" action of a black man on my neighborhood block, I was serving (naively) as a guardian of white privilege and racial segregation. A norm had been broken, an expectation had been violated, and I was demanding an explanation. Like a police officer on patrol, I jumped into action when I witnessed an infraction. I may not have established the norms of segregation, but I was, unintentionally, contributing to their reproduction.

At the same time, it is important to recognize that the reproduction of inequality is not inevitable. Oppressive social institutions and dominating social practices may have momentum, but no social structure is ever predestined. All of us possess some level of independence and agency from the forces of inequality, which is to say; positive social change is always on the horizon of possibilities. At the very same time that racial segregation was being reproduced in my Seattle neighborhood, activists in my community were organizing, agitating, resisting, and pushing back against the forces of exclusion and inequality. As a result, state and local laws were eventually changed, racist beliefs and assumptions gradually subsided, and today, I doubt that a young white child in my old neighborhood would react with astonishment at the sight of an African American walking down the street. Resistance and reproduction represent opposing sides in a skirmish that takes place on multiple battlefields. Some are momentary scuffles that dissolve in seconds, while others are long-standing wars that last for generations. In both instances, however, the outcome is a matter of power.

Power

One basic understanding of power is that it is simply the ability of an individual or group to control other individuals or groups. In this sense, power and inequality are like two sides of the same coin—one cannot exist without the other. The more power a group has, the more it is able to secure valuable resources, and the more resources a group has, the more power it gains. It makes little sense to try and separate the two concepts. At some level, power differences in a society are inevitable, and it would be naïve to think that equality in all aspects of our lives is even possible. In fact, in some circumstances complete equality may not even be desirable. The control that parents have over their young children and the authority of teachers over students are examples of unequal power relationships that are accepted as legitimate and beneficial. But sometimes the power to control another person is also used to dominate and exploit, as when a parent physically abuses a child, or a teacher sexually harasses a student. In such circumstances, inequality and the concentration of power are harmful and destructive.

One particularly disturbing problem with inequality is that we do not always recognize domination and exploitation when we see it. We often accept differences in power as beneficial when they are in fact doing harm. And we sometimes consent to domination despite its destructive consequences. Powerful groups ignore the fact that they are privileged, while powerless groups are discouraged from exploring the source of their exploitation.

Growing up as a white person in Seattle, I did not know that my skin color allowed me the privilege of living west of Twenty-Third Avenue. My family never pointed to the racial segregation of my neighborhood as a problem, my teachers did not identify it as a harmful act, and it wasn't addressed from the pulpit at my church. I may have been told that whites and blacks were persons of equal worth and value, but my everyday experience suggested otherwise. In my all-white neighborhood, the streets were lined with large oak and chestnut trees, the single-family houses were freshly painted, the schools and parks were within walking distance, and late-model cars were parked on the curb. In the black neighborhood, however, there were more apartment buildings, the houses were worn down, the corner grocery stores were smaller and less attractive, there were fewer trees and more noise, and the cars were usually older and in disrepair.

The point I am trying to make here is that the relationship between inequality and power is complex. Domination can occur at multiple levels, and exploitation is often unrecognized and unchallenged. Individual attitudes, social interaction, and cultural traditions work hand in hand with economic systems, political organizations, educational institutions, and religious groups to protect the powerful and legitimate a system of social exclusion, privilege, and discrimination. It is a system that is reinforced by rules that are created and enforced by the powerful.

Rules

Many different types of rules regulate our social life. Some rules are formal, clearly articulated, and enforced by a recognizable official. The rules of sport meet these criteria. College basketball, for example, is governed by a formal rulebook with detailed descriptions of permitted behavior and associated penalties for violations. Trained referees are hired to officiate the game and determine fair play. A player with too many rule violations will be removed from the game and maybe—if the violations are severe and intentional—even suspended for several games. The same holds true for the rules that are created by a legislative body. If you violate the federal tax code and refuse to pay your legally mandated share of taxes, there is a good chance you will be arrested, tried for your crime, and sent to prison.

Some rules, on the other hand, are informal, do not appear in an official document, and are enforced in a more casual manner. The rules that regulate appropriate dress and table manners, as well as the rules governing greetings and conversations, fall under this category. If you refuse to shake an extended hand or constantly interrupt a speaker, others might criticize you to your face or gossip about you behind your back, but there is no formally regulated sanction associated with the violation of informal rules. The experience of feeling humiliated or shamed might correct your rude behavior, but no officer or referee is assigned to enforce informal rules.

Both informal and formal rules are used to maintain patterns of inequality. For example, as a young boy, I contributed to the racial segregation of my all-white neighborhood by noticing and calling out the "nonwhite rule-breaker" on my street. My role as a guardian of racial segregation may seem inconsequential, but the informal rules of inequality are often enforced unintentionally with actions that seem small and insignificant. When powerful people come to expect deference from the powerless, they are reminding others of an informal rule that works to their advantage, and when less powerful individuals adopt a subservient demeanor, they too are acknowledging that the informal rule works in favor of the powerful.

Formal rules that advantage one group over another are easier to detect and often easier to eliminate. In the case of residential segregation in Seattle, there were numerous laws and codes that were intentionally created to ensure the separation of whites and blacks. Influential real estate developers, real estate agents, and city officials were engaged in a conspiracy to exclude blacks from purchasing or renting homes in certain Seattle neighborhoods, mostly because it benefited them financially and politically. This strategy of exploitation was legally codified in 1926 when the following covenant was attached to the deed of every home in my old neighborhood: "No part of the lands owned by him or described following their signatures of this instrument shall ever be used or occupied by or sold, conveyed, leased, rented, or given to negroes, or any person or person of the negro blood."[6]

In addition, the local "Realtors Code of Ethics" that was in place at the time mandated that no person should be sold a house if the person's race or nationality would be expected to reduce property values. Thus, discrimination in housing was not only considered good business, but it was also considered ethical by the standards of the (white) profession.

Both the informal and formal rules that structured the buying, selling, and renting of houses in Seattle were discriminatory and rigged in advance to favor a certain class of people; namely, those with "white" identities. Using identity as a factor in the allocation of valued resources is another core feature of inequality.

Identity

There is wide agreement among social scientists that human social interaction is unique in that most of our communication occurs with and through the use of symbols. Unlike dogs, apes, birds, fish, and other animals, humans have developed elaborate languages, systems of writing and reading, forms of artistic expression, and detailed moral codes that emerge from shared symbols. One particularly important feature of this evolutionary capacity is that humans are capable of inventing symbolic markers to label, categorize, classify, and identify each other. Once established, these linguistic categories are then used to determine each other's identity.

I may be an absolutely unique person, but my individuality is defined in terms of common, socially recognizable categories linked to my occupation, marital status, age, criminal history, health, skin color, height, weight, nationality, sexual orientation, and other identity classifications. In other words, as human beings we interpret and understand our social world using identity markers associated with a range of different categories that are, for one reason or another, considered important in our society. This is a learned skill, which means that the categories we accept and recognize as important are those that have been taught to us by others in our community. As we mature and gain more diverse experiences, our understanding of identity categories becomes more elaborate and nuanced, but we never stop using identity labels as the foundation for understanding who we are and who others are.

When I was six years old I had familiarity with a relatively small number of identity categories, and most of these were associated with family, friends, school, and neighborhood. For example, I understood male-female and mother-father, but I would have been confused by same-sex parenting since it violated my narrow experience with these identities. I had knowledge of basic occupational categories such as "mailman," "garbageman," "doctor," and "priest," but I would have been incredulous if a woman appeared in any of these roles. And like

other children my age, the meanings associated with these person classifications were rather narrow and unsophisticated. I did not understand that the garbage collector had less prestige and status than the
doctor. In my mind, a job that required riding in a huge truck was more
desirable than one that involved looking down throats and giving injec-
tions with scary looking needles.

By the age of six, I had learned to associate the identity category
"negro" with skin color and geography. I was unaware of the pejorative
and harmful meanings that were linked to this label by most white
people—that understanding would come with time. Through the process of socialization, we expand our vocabulary of socially recognized
identities and gradually adopt the prevailing meanings associated with
these categories. In this way, we come to understand that some persons
have more value and power than other persons, and we also come to
understand that our own identity is subject to similar evaluations of
worth and influence. Man-woman, black-white, gay-straight, employee-
owner, are not simply categories that recognize difference; they are also
the symbolic means for doing inequality.

STRUCTURE OF THE BOOK

I have organized the chapters of this book around five questions:

1. What is inequality?
2. What does identity have to do with inequality?
3. How does identity contribute to the reproduction of inequality?
4. How is identity used to resist inequality?
5. What is the relationship between micro inequality and macro
   inequality?

Here it is important to emphasize a point that will be made throughout
all five chapters: Devalued identities are neither a fundamental cause of
inequality nor are they inconsequential byproducts of economic and
political forces. Rather, the central theme of this book is that *the making and breaking of inequality depends upon and operates through a
complex set of identity categories and identity processes.* These processes have been recognized and acknowledged by sociologists and social

psychologists for some time. Up to this point, however, they have not been systematically reviewed and integrated in a manner that is both academically sound while also being accessible to a more general public. That is my intent with this volume.

I

WHAT IS INEQUALITY?

Many years ago I was having lunch with some colleagues at my university when our conversation turned to the topic of inequality. This was not a formal academic debate by any means, and as I recall, the discussion was sparked by a report comparing the average salary of top college administrators to the average salary of college professors. The study showed that the take-home pay for our bosses (the administrators) was more than three times the salary of an average professor. Our lunch table included faculty from various departments across campus, and as one might expect, my colleagues voiced a good deal of anger and frustration in learning about the pay gap. "What could possibly justify such a huge difference in compensation?" we asked. To most of us at the lunch table this was clear evidence of an unfair distribution of university resources, and it needed to be changed. There was, however, one voice of dissent. A friend of mine from the biology department was visibly restrained and did not join in our collective display of righteous indignation—and it was not because she aspired to someday become an administrator. Rather, her reasoning was simple and straightforward: "Inequality is inevitable, it is natural to our species, and we should come to expect it."

I remember thinking that she had a point. In its most basic form, inequality is simply the establishment of rank or status among individuals or categories of individuals within a social group, and off the top of my head I could not think of a single social species that did not have some type of dominance or status hierarchy. I am not an expert on animal social behavior, but my colleague was, and she provided numerous examples of how systems of rank or status are established within the so-called animal kingdom. Moreover, she was not surprised that we were all generally upset at failing to win the top position in our group's dominance hierarchy. As she pointed out, in most species, one's status is usually the outcome of an aggressive act or dispute over a scarce resource such as territory or a mating partner.

Many types of birds, for example, will establish a pecking order in competition over food, and chickens have been known to produce a distinct and recognizable line of power in a flock of up to twenty birds. While other species may not engage in the actual act of pecking, they do use similar forms of "agonistic behavior" to determine each other's relative value. Sometimes dominance is linked to an animal's age, size, or gender, but other times vocalizations, odors, or visual displays will be used to signal intelligence, strength, and power.

We see this, for example, in wolf packs where the so-called alpha male displays his superior position during interaction with subordinates by standing erect, inflating his chest, and raising his ears, while at the same time gazing toward the distance in a pose of regal superiority. Wolves that have accepted their lower status within the pack will acknowledge their inferior position by crouching low to the ground in a submissive pose while gently nuzzling the chin and lips of the alpha. If a defiant competitor refuses to engage in the deferential display demanded by the leader of the pack, a physical confrontation will often ensue and the winner of the fight will earn the top rank. In a similar manner, bighorn rams will determine their relative value by displaying the size and curl of their horns—the bigger the horns, the higher the status. When rank is contested, the competitors will engage in a violent clashing of skulls until a victor is determined. The fiercest battles will occur between rams of equal size, and these scuffles sometimes result in serious injury and even death.

But violent physical battles are not always necessary; some species have evolved forms of ritual display that serve as a threat or scare tactic in place of an actual fight. This is the case for peacocks that use the color and size of their feather plumage as a signal of dominance. When looking for a mate, peahens will be attracted to males with the most colorful, flamboyant, and ornate display of tail feathers. And while these examples suggest that males are more likely to dominate women in the animal kingdom, this is not always the case. Spotted hyena social groups are led by females who are typically larger and stronger than males, elephant troops also have a matriarchal structure that forces young males out of the group once they mature. One of the more interesting gender-based dominance hierarchies is found in the dwarf angelfish where a single male rules a harem of two to six females. However, if the male is killed or otherwise disappears, the least subordinate female will assume the dominant position, but only after she first changes gender and becomes a male.

Perhaps the most relevant comparison to our own species is found in the way chimpanzees establish dominance. This should not be surprising given that great apes are considered to be the closest to humans in terms of intelligence and behavior. Consider, for example, how Jane Goodall, the famous primatologist, described the manner in which a young and ambitious male chimp (she named him Mike) employed a newly discovered tool in his quest to become the leader of his community. This episode took place in the jungles of Tanzania where Goodall and her companion and future husband, Hugo van Lawick, had set up camp in an attempt to gain access to chimpanzee social life. Up to this point, Mike was near the bottom of the dominance hierarchy, was threatened and attacked by other males, and was always the last in line to retrieve bananas.

> All at once Mike calmly walked over to our tent and took hold of an empty kerosene can by the handle. Then he picked up a second can and, walking upright, returned to the place where he had been sitting. Armed with his two cans Mike continued to stare toward the other males. After a few minutes he began to rock from side to side. At first the movement was almost imperceptible, but Hugo and I were watching him closely. Gradually he rocked more vigorously, his hair slowly began to stand erect, and then, softly at first, he started a series of pant-hoots. As he called, Mike got to his feet and suddenly he was off, charging toward the group of males, hitting the two cans ahead of him. The cans, together with Mike's crescendo of hooting, made the most appalling racket: no wonder the erstwhile peaceful males rushed out of the way. Mike and his cans vanished down a track, and after a few moments there was silence. Some of the males reassembled and resumed their interrupted grooming session, but the others stood around somewhat apprehensively.[1]

Mike's tactic proved to be very effective as he eventually established himself as first in rank for his group. And because no other chimps were able to use objects made by humans with such deliberate and intentional skill, Goodall attributed Mike's rise in status to his superior intelligence:

> Charging displays usually occur at a time of emotional excitement— when a chimpanzee arrives at a food source, joins up with another group, or when he is frustrated. But it seemed that Mike actually planned his charging displays; almost, one might say, in cold blood.[2]

We must be careful not to anthropomorphize animal behavior and project our own human interpretations and motivations onto other species, but it is true, nevertheless, that inequality in animal groups is nearly ubiquitous. On this point my colleague in the biology department was correct. Our species is not unique when it comes to establishing social structures of inequality. However, her claim that inequality is therefore "inevitable" is a different issue altogether. In fact, the biological evidence shows us that status hierarchies in nature are not fixed structures, nor do they represent the simple unfolding of permanent genetic codes. Instead, there is an emerging consensus among experts in the field that social dominance in animal groups is shaped in part by changing environmental conditions, and is also partly the product of social interaction and communication about social status.[3] Biology matters for sure, but it is only one component of a much larger set of processes.

But even more to the point is the anthropological evidence regarding our own species. There is no doubt that most human groups today are characterized by the unequal distribution of valued resources—the salary gap between professors and administrators is only one of many obvious examples. However, for most of human history our species has in fact lived cooperatively in largely egalitarian social structures and in groups where dominant alpha leaders did not exist. This was especially the case more than twelve thousand years ago when so-called foraging societies were most prevalent. In these small communities, families survived by gathering edible plants and hunting wild game. They rarely had permanent dwellings and would instead move their camps in response to seasonal variation in food sources. It was not until the invention of agriculture and the domestication of livestock that we begin to see the emergence of gender hierarchies, despotic leaders, chiefdoms, and institutionalized forms of slavery.[4] In other words, the fact that our species cooperated for tens of thousands of years and thrived under relatively egalitarian social structures, shows that for humans, at least, a dominance hierarchy is neither natural nor inevitable. On this point my friend the biologist was simply wrong.

But this raises another question: Can we assume that our species is "naturally" altruistic and that modern society has somehow corrupted our inherent preference for equality, peace, and harmony? This is the influential argument of Jean-Jacques Rousseau, the eighteenth-century Romantic philosopher who believed that in the state of nature "the savage lives within himself," unconcerned with the opinions of others and unmotivated by status and power.[5] Rousseau was writing before Darwin's theory of evolution and without the benefit of advanced anthropological and archeological research. We now know that the evolutionary development of inequality in our species followed a more circuitous path, one that did not include a stage of natural altruism, freedom, and independence.

It appears that our earliest human ancestors were very much like our great ape cousins of today. The very first human social groups, those that existed thirty thousand to forty thousand years ago, were characterized by a despotic hierarchy of dominance. These were not the noble savages imagined by some early philosophers. There was competition for status, displays of power, and physical confrontations that likely resulted in injury and maybe even death. At some point in time, however, we invented a primitive system of equal exchange and cooperation based on cultural rules that kept individual attempts at power in check. This is the conclusion, at least, that renowned anthropologist Christopher Boehm reached in his extensive review of the scientific evidence.[6] And today most scholars agree that hunters and gatherers had to stamp out individual battles for dominance if they were to succeed.

According to Boehm, this first began when a coalition of subordinates learned how to band together to control the power plays of alpha individuals—a form of "reverse dominance." Eventually others would copy the initial success of these small groups until the entire community agreed to guard against the aggressive tendencies of upstart alphas (like Mike the chimp). This of course is a dramatically abbreviated version of the story, and we must acknowledge that it is a theory and somewhat speculative, but Boehm's evidence is compelling. At some point our ancestors discovered the advantages of egalitarian cooperation and learned how to create a set of moral rules that banned despotic leaders. Importantly, it is at this precise juncture in the evolution of our species that we begin to distinguish ourselves from great apes.

We share many traits and predispositions with other animal species, and we now know that human intelligence is not as "superior" as was once thought. In fact, on certain tests of memory, apes consistently outperform humans. We also know chimpanzees, orangutans, and gorillas use tools in their natural habitat and have learned to communicate using sign language while in captivity. We even have evidence that apes have a sense of self, or at least the ability to recognize themselves as unique beings in the world, which is a prerequisite for learning how to plan actions, strategize, and invent. Still, these skills are rudimentary in comparison to those of a typical human. While apes can learn signs, they can't learn to read, create their own language, or teach sign language to other apes. Because of our more highly advanced capacity to use symbols, humans can have conversations about events in the past, analyze abstract ideas, and discuss plans for the future, all of which depend upon language. And language, it turns out, is a uniquely powerful weapon, mightier than the physical strength of an alpha male and more effective than the clanging of empty kerosene cans.

It is through the use of language that a coalition of subordinates is able to create a stable set of moral principles for the purpose of curbing the ambitions of an aspiring alpha. We find inequalities of power and privilege in most every animal social structure, but only humans have the ability to create a vision of an ideal society and intentionally redesign social life using a common set of moral and political guidelines. Chimps and bonobos clearly engage in cooperative behavior, they display evidence of empathy, and they will initiate rituals of reconciliation after a conflict, but only humans have been known to construct complex economic organizations, political institutions, and religious bodies that reproduce and challenge inequality. Only humans have fashioned schools for learning science, art, and philosophy. And only humans have been able to build a culture where individuals are classified, evaluated, ranked, rewarded, and punished using symbolic categories of social identity.[7]

For this reason, inequality in human societies is more than the simple establishment of rank or status among individuals in competition with each other. In our species, inequality is also associated with a range of cultural, economic, and political rules for allocating more resources to some people and less to others; it depends upon the creation of powerful social institutions where domination and exploitation are legitimated, and it involves the use of symbols and identities where individuals are linked to social categories with differing amounts of value, power, and privilege. Because of this unique complexity, sociologists agree that the study of inequality in human societies should occur at several different levels.[8] We might, for example, examine patterns of resource distribution across different geographical regions and social categories of people and ask, "Which groups and individuals receive the most income, wealth, education, political power, and respect? Who has the best physical and mental health, and who receives the best care and attention when sick?" We might want to dissect the different cultural, economic, and political rules for distributing valued resources and ask, "Who makes the rules? Who benefits from the rules? How are the rules enforced and changed?" And finally, we might want to scrutinize the micro-level processes of face-to-face interactions and ask, "Why do some identity categories have less value and less power than others? What are the personal and interpersonal consequences of being defined by a devalued and degraded identity category? Why do identity-based inequalities persist?"

In the next section I will take a closer look at the different ways in which inequality is found in human society and offer some concrete examples of its manifestation at several overlapping levels of analysis.

LAYERS OF INEQUALITY

Maxine Hanley is having her picture taken for a newspaper article about her life. She is a beautiful woman in her mid-fifties with a full, round face, and high cheekbones. With her auburn hair pulled back and her dark eyes slightly narrowed, she appears sincere and gentle, like a caring friend or a sympathetic grandmother. Still, there is uneasiness in her smile. In fact, it is hard to tell whether it is a smile at all. Her lips are parted just enough to see her teeth, but the corners of her mouth do not turn upward. The photographer may have caught Maxine in an awkward pose, but the image may also reflect a sense of apprehension and uncertainty with the spotlight of public attention.

For most of her life, Maxine has lived in fear. She was sexually assaulted and emotionally abused by family members. As the oldest of three children, she took on the responsibility of caring for and protecting her younger siblings. Her parents were heavy drinkers, and physical violence was common in her home. At the age of eighteen she left the chaos and hostility of her place of birth and never looked back. Once out of the house, she too started to drink and soon fell into the same pattern of alcohol abuse she witnessed as a child. For most of the next thirty years, Maxine was homeless, moving from town to town and living on the streets while drinking up to three pints of hard liquor a day. Sadly, the same violence that she tried to escape as a teenager haunted her in the alleys, camps, and shelters of her adopted towns.

On this day, however, Maxine is safe and sober. With the support of friends and professional counselors, she survived the grueling process of detoxification, secured transitional housing, and began sharing her story of recovery with other homeless people. At the time of the newspaper article, Maxine was taking college classes with the hope of becoming a registered nurse.[9]

In most every city and town in America there are men, women, and children who are living a life similar to Maxine's. We can find them sleeping in cars or sidewalks, panhandling on street corners, or crowding into social service shelters in search of food, warmth, and safety. The homeless among us are a stark reminder of the gap between the haves and the have-nots in society, and when a disheveled and desperate panhandler approaches a well-groomed business executive on a busy downtown street, we are confronted with the visible reality of inequality.

Inequality in modern human societies is diverse and is found in many different forms. Sometimes it is obvious in our everyday encounters with neighbors, friends, and family who lack the basic resources needed for survival. Other times, however, it is more subtle, and may reflect accepted differences in power and authority, as when an employee takes orders from a boss, a military general is saluted by a lower-ranking officer, or a religious leader directs a congregation. But other structures of inequality are more highly concealed and rarely observed. For example, the stock value of a corporation, the military power of a nation-state, and the prestige of a religious denomination are not qualities of individuals, but are, nevertheless, important dimensions of inequality. Military power, business wealth, prestige, and respect are but a few of the many types of assets that can be earned, owned, controlled, won, lost, stolen, depleted, or hoarded in society. Economic resources usually come to mind when we think of inequality (e.g., cash, stocks, bonds, real estate), but other physical objects (e.g., weapons, food, shelter), qualities associated with a person's body (health, physical strength, athletic skill), as well as more abstract symbols and representations of power and privilege are also important (e.g., knowledge, education, respect, prestige).

Because there are so many different types of valued resources in society, and because they can be represented in so many ways, there is a range of different approaches to the measurement and analysis of inequality. One might, for example, focus on the variable distribution of resources between large groups, such as social classes and nation-states, explore how economic inequality has changed over time, and investigate the antagonisms and conflicts generated by inequality. This is the approach that was famously taken by Karl Marx and more recently by Thomas Piketty and others who have investigated the variable distribution of capital in the modern political economy. Another option might be to examine the unequal distribution of power, status, wealth, and income across different occupations, political parties, and organizations. We see this, for example, in the classic work of Max Weber and more recent studies of the so-called power elite by the likes of C. Wright Mills and G. William Domhoff. Or one might conduct a more narrowly focused analysis of how inequality is experienced in the everyday lives of persons who are categorized using degraded social identities, such as unemployed black men; single, working mothers; or Latino immigrants. This is the strategy adopted by skilled ethnographic researchers such as Katherine Newman and Elijah Anderson.[10]

The point here is that there is no one way to study inequality. Different strategies have different strengths and limitations, and often reflect different levels of analysis. A macro-analysis of inequality between nations or regions of the world is just as important as a micro-analysis of inequality within a small group. While scholars tend to specialize in one level to the exclusion of others, this does not detract from the fact that the different layers of inequality remain parts of an integrated whole.

Thus, the particulars of Maxine Hanley's life—the violence in her family, her struggle with addiction, and her life on the streets—are not
independent of larger social forces. It is easy to imagine that Maxine's
life was also impacted by employment opportunities in a regional economy, the quality of local political and educational institutions, as well as
the cultural and political rules governing gender, race, and social class.

One relatively simple and common way to get a picture of the layers
of inequality is to examine differences in average income. As we all
know, some people work jobs, own businesses, or have access to invest-
ments that provide relatively large sums of cash on a regular basis.
Others, however, are either unemployed, have low-paying jobs, or have
no access to investment income. The story of Maxine is illustrative of a
person who has struggled to live a life with very few valued resources:
no housing, no employment, no savings, limited food, poor health, little
in the way of status or respect, and of course, no income. Understanding who receives more or less income can, therefore, provide a very
rough approximation of inequality. Similarly, when household earnings
are calculated for different groups, we can see how income is associated
with group identity. We know, for example, that men on average make
more than women. College graduates on average make more than high
school dropouts. White people make more on average than nonwhites.

Some group differences in income may be obvious and predictable—infants have lower incomes than adults—but other group differences will be less apparent and more worthy of sociological analysis.
Table 1.1, for example, shows how income is distributed around the
globe by comparing the top ten countries with the bottom ten countries.

Here the difference is striking. The residents of countries with the
highest average income per household took in over $50,000 per year,
while those living in countries with the lowest income received less than
$1,000 per year, on average. When similar figures for all countries are
plotted on a map of the world, a clear pattern emerges: The highest
incomes are in Europe, North America, and Australia, while the lowest
incomes appear mostly in Africa and parts of Asia and Latin America.

This simple analysis shows that household income is not evenly distributed between nation-states. A person's chances of being poor or rich
are much greater in some countries than in others. But what makes this
fact even more notable is that a very similar geographic pattern appears

Table 1.1. Average Household Income by Country

Top Ten Countries		Bottom Ten Countries	
Luxembourg	$52,493	Burundi	$673
Norway	$51,489	Liberia	$781
Sweden	$50,514	Madagascar	$1,013
Australia	$46,555	Rwanda	$1,101
Denmark	$44,360	Zambia	$1,501
United States	$43,585	Benin	$1,502
Canada	$41,280	Burkina Faso	$1,530
Netherlands	$38,584	Togo	$1,571
Finland	$34,615	Mali	$1,983
Germany	$33,333	Sierra Leone	$2,330

Note: Figures are aggregated data collected by Gallup, Inc., from 2006 to 2012 and are based on responses from at least two thousand adults in each country. For measurement details see Glenn Phelps and Steve Crabtree, "Worldwide, Median Household Income About $10,000," Gallup, December 16, 2013, http://www.gallup.com/poll/166211/worldwide-median-household-income -000.aspx#2.

when we map other valuable resources and life outcomes, such a household wealth, average years of formal education, rates of hunger, access to health care, and overall life expectancy. A typical baby born today in Luxembourg or Norway will not only earn one of the highest incomes in the world, but also will likely experience many years of formal education and live a long and healthy life. On the other hand, a baby born in Burundi or Liberia has a greater chance of living a short, sickly life characterized by poverty, hunger, and limited education.

A cursory examination of the figures in table 1.1 clearly shows that the nation-state is a factor in income inequality. For this reason, it is critical that we try to explain the uneven distribution of valued resources that exists between different regions of the world. But this is only one analytical layer; we must also be mindful of patterns of inequality that simultaneously exist within political boundaries of rich and poor countries.

The United States, for example, is by most every economic measure one of the richest countries in the world. It has the most productive economy, the world's largest military budget, the sixth highest average income (as seen in table 1.1), and it is home to over forty-five thousand "ultramillionaires"—those with a net worth of more than $50 million. But as we all know, not everyone in the United States is rich, and there are regions in the country where thousands of people live in poverty.

We can get a very fuzzy snapshot of regional inequality within the United States by comparing average income of different counties. Table 1.2 shows the ten counties with the lowest average income as well as the ten counties with the highest average income. Here we can see that the difference between counties is actually greater than the difference between countries. The richest counties have average family incomes of more than $100,000 a year, while the poorest counties have family incomes well below $30,000 a year.

This is a dramatic difference and a stark illustration of income inequality within a very wealthy nation. South Dakota and Virginia, the states where the poorest and richest counties are located, are 1,500 miles apart, so it might be tempting to conclude that income differences are a reflection of regional geography. But similar differences between counties can also be found within the same state. Take New Mexico, for example, where Los Alamos County has a median household income of $107,126, the sixth highest in the nation, whereas McKinley County, only one hundred miles to the west, has an average income of only $29,040.

Anyone familiar with New Mexico would likely offer an "obvious" explanation for the discrepancy in household income between the two counties: Los Alamos County is the site of the Los Alamos National Laboratory, a federal research facility that employs more than nine thousand scientists and associated staff who are highly educated and generously compensated. McKinley County, on the other hand, encom-

Table 1.2. Average Household Income by US Counties

Top Ten Counties		Bottom Ten Counties	
Loudoun County (VA)	$125,900	Buffalo County (SD)	$22,894
Falls Church city (VA)	$122,092	Wilcox County (AL)	$23,014
Fairfax County (VA)	$112,844	Owsley County (KY)	$23,341
Howard County (MD)	$110,224	Bell County (KY)	$23,968
Douglas County (CO)	$109,926	Clay County (KY)	$24,001
Los Alamos County (NM)	$107,126	Holmes County (MS)	$24,065
Williamson County (TN)	$104,367	Greene County (AL)	$25,398
Arlington County (VA)	$104,354	Humphreys County (MS)	$25,625
Hunterdon County (NJ)	$102,797	McCreary County (KY)	$25,655
Morris County (NJ)	$101,754	Sumter County (AL)	$25,931

Source: "Small Area Income and Poverty Estimates (SAIPE)," Census.gov, 2015, https://www.census.gov/did/www/saipe/data/interactive/saipe.html.
Note: Figures are US Census Bureau estimates for 2015.

passes parts of the Navajo Nation and the Pueblo of Zuni Reservation, and as a consequence, 75 percent of the county's seventy thousand residents are Native American. Locals would not be surprised to learn, therefore, that over 30 percent of McKinley County residents live in poverty while less than 3 percent of Los Alamos County families fall below the poverty line. To put it more bluntly, scientists are more likely to have high incomes, and Native Americans are more likely to have low incomes. But this observation is not an explanation.

Knowing the social identities of the county residents might help us "make sense" of regional differences in average income, but it does not answer the more fundamental question: Why do so many Native Americans in McKinley County live in poverty? Or more generally, why are American Indian people throughout the United States more likely to be poor? Indeed, if we take a closer look at the US counties with the highest rate of poverty, we see that half of the bottom ten counties have populations that are a majority Native American. And when we drill down even further, we find that persons who identify exclusively as American Indian or Alaskan Native have a poverty rate of 29 percent (in 2012), which is nearly three times the poverty rate for individuals who identify as white (11 percent).

When low incomes, high unemployment, and poverty are dispropor-tionately associated with a particular group for a long period of time (as has been the case for Native people in the United States), it often comes to be accepted as tolerable or even normal. It is tantamount to saying, "Native American people are poor because they are Native American." But the variable distribution of valued resources is neither random nor natural. It is usually the direct, and sometimes indirect, consequence of intentional human behavior. A more complete under-standing of the disproportionate exploitation of Native American peo-ple, therefore, requires a much more elaborate investigation of the rules, practices, and resources used to create and maintain this particu-lar form of inequality. This might include, for example, a historical analysis of European colonialism, a political analysis of American terri-torial expansion and policies of genocide, an institutional analysis of the Bureau of Indian Affairs, an economic analysis of capitalist expansion and exclusion, as well as a cultural analysis of prejudice and discrimina-tion.

Finally, when we peel away enough layers of society, we eventually encounter actual humans engaged in routine, everyday practices. While many aspects of our customary behaviors may seem mundane and insignificant, they are, nevertheless, part of an intricate web of interactions that impact the health, dignity, and happiness of us all. Which brings us back to Maxine Hanley, whose story of abuse, addiction, and recovery was reported in an investigative series on poverty and violence suffered by Native peoples living in urban areas. Maxine is from the Navajo Nation in McKinley County, New Mexico. And while her personal journey is unique, it is also illustrative of the disproportionate hardships that threaten many American Indians. Journalist Nick Estes, the author of the investigative series, reports that Native people experience twice as much violence as any other ethnic group, and at least one in three indigenous women are raped in their lifetime. Native people are also four times more likely to be sent to prison when arrested, and native youth are twice as likely to be admitted to an adult prison.

Jackie McKinney, the mayor of Gallup, New Mexico (also in McKinley County) believes that the problem of homelessness and alcoholism among Natives is simply a matter of poor decision making: "Drinking alcohol is a choice of every individual" and "these people are not making the right choices."[11] What Mayor McKinney fails to understand, however, is that some people have more choices, more options, and more opportunities than others. By reducing the problem of poverty, drugs, and homelessness to individual choice, the mayor is dismissing our collective responsibilities and affirming centuries-old stereotypes of Native people. The pejorative image of the drunken Indian obscures the fact that the vast majority of Native Americans are neither homeless nor addicted to alcohol. On the other hand, exploitation, discrimination, and inequality are common to almost every person with an indigenous identity. As Estes notes, "Spanish and Anglo colonization and histories of brutality reverberate well into the present, especially against the city's indigenous population." Indeed, it is quite likely that Maxine Hanley's life was disrupted by the very same historical aftershocks.

The basic premise of this book is that degraded social identities are central to understanding inequality. The identity labels of "homeless," "Indian," and "woman," for example, are not simply neutral words for classifying and talking about groups of people. Identity labels affect the way we think, they influence our understanding of self, they shape our perceptions of each other, they guide our plans for action; they are used to justify power, to establish public policy, and to organize social change. To be sure, identity processes do not operate in isolation, and we should not forget that economic, political, and cultural systems are key to the production of inequality. But these larger social processes are themselves dependent upon our unique ability to name and label each other. In the next chapter I will provide a more in-depth explanation of identity, explore the different ways in which identity is experienced, and further elaborate on the way in which identity is part of inequality.

2

WHAT DOES IDENTITY HAVE TO DO WITH INEQUALITY?

In their most elementary form, *identities* are simply category labels that we use to name ourselves and the people around us. They are recognizable in the words that we use every day to introduce ourselves, talk about our family, and describe the people in our lives. Some identity categories are used to classify social relationships (e.g., married, mother, friend); some refer to our job, religion, or political affiliation (e.g., barista, Jewish, Republican); some are focused on physical characteristics (e.g., gender, race) or personal qualities (e.g., intelligence, mood); others reference past actions (e.g., ex-con, retired police officer); and some reference more nuanced category labels tied to small groups or informal slang (e.g., team captain, wimp). Generally, to the extent that a category label can be used to identify, classify, or indicate a person as a certain type, it can serve as an identity.

At the same time, it is important to emphasize that an identity is a unique type of category label. In real-world interaction, an identity label cannot be treated as arbitrary or essentially subjective, dismissed as irrelevant or random, or ignored without serious social consequences. This is because identities exist in social relationships, are central to the structure of modern society, are deeply embedded in our social institutions, and are fundamental to how we organize social life. They have the power to enable and constrain the thoughts, emotions, and actions of real persons. This is especially true for identities that are associated with an unequal distribution of valued resources.

Consider, for example, the categories "male" and "female." It would be difficult to argue that these two identities are arbitrary category labels. It is obvious to anyone with minimal life experience that these two words are embodied in the human physiology of sex and procreation and reflect dominant cultural norms associated with fashion, family structure, religious tradition, and public policy. Most importantly for our purposes, gender identities are linked to social segregation, discrimination, exploitation, and inequality. Gender identity is so firmly entrenched in our social structure, and so fundamental to social relations, that even if we tried somehow to live a genderless life, others would "do gender" for us. This point is poignantly illustrated by sociologist Betsy Lucal, who uses her unique life experience to reveal the power and rigidity of gender categories:[1]

> Each day, I negotiate the boundaries of gender. Each day, I face the possibility that someone will attribute the "wrong" gender to me based on my physical appearance. I am six feet tall and large-boned. I have had short hair for most of my life. For the past several years, I have worn a crew cut or flat top. I do not shave or otherwise remove hair from my body (e.g., no eyebrow plucking). I do not wear dresses, skirts, high heels, or makeup. My only jewelry is a class ring, a "men's" watch (my wrists are too large for a "women's" watch), two small earrings (gold hoops, both in my left ear), and (occasionally) a necklace. I wear jeans or shorts, T-shirts, sweaters, polo/golf shirts, button-down collar shirts, and tennis shoes or boots. The jeans are "women's" (I do have hips) but do not look particularly "feminine." The rest of the outer garments are from men's departments. I prefer baggy clothes, so the fact that I have "womanly" breasts often is not obvious (I do not wear a bra). Sometimes, I wear a baseball cap or some other type of hat. I also am white and relatively young (30 years old).
>
> I am female; I self-identify as a woman. I do not claim to be some other gender or to have no gender at all. I simply place myself in the wrong category according to stereotypes and cultural standards; the gender I present, or that some people perceive me to be presenting, is inconsistent with the gender with which I identify myself as well as with the gender I could be "proven" to be. Socially, I display the wrong gender; personally, I identify as the proper gender.

Because gender identity is strictly defined as either male or female, and because gender is central to the construction of our social relationships and embedded in the structure of our social institutions, the violation of expectations regarding wardrobe and hairstyle can have serious social consequences. This is especially true for those situations where social norms demand segregation. While Professor Lucal may be comfortable with her more flexible display of gender, she recognizes that it can create confusion and fear in other people's lives. As a result, she has learned to anticipate and accommodate the anxiety of others:

> In general, in unfamiliar public places, I avoid using the rest room because I know that it is a place where there is a high likelihood of misattribution and where misattribution is socially important. If I must use a public rest room, I try to make myself look as nonthreatening as possible. I do not wear a hat, and I try to rearrange my clothing to make my breasts more obvious. Here, I am trying to use my secondary sex characteristics to make my gender more obvious rather than the usual use of gender to make sex obvious. While in the rest room, I never make eye contact, and I get in and out as quickly as possible. Going in with a woman friend also is helpful; her presence legitimizes my own. People are less likely to think I am entering a space where I do not belong when I am with someone who looks like she does belong. To those women who verbally challenge my presence in the rest room, I reply, "I know," usually in an annoyed tone. When they stare or talk about me to the women they are with, I simply get out as quickly as possible. In general, I do not wait for someone I am with because there is too much chance of an unpleasant encounter. I stopped trying on clothes before purchasing them a few years ago because my presence in the changing areas was met with stares and whispers.

The experience of Betsy Lucal demonstrates how challenging it can be to live on the boundaries between identity categories. We know that the meaning of *male* and *female* varies across cultures and changes with time, and that the expectations for appropriate dress and hair length are not written in stone. Similarly, the rules for sex segregation are also quite different across cultures. In Saudi Arabia, for example, women and men are segregated in public schools, they pray in separate sections of the mosque, they are usually segregated in public restaurants, and they very often have separate rooms within the household. This is obviously a far cry from the United States, where gender segregation in public and private places is minimal. But Professor Lucal's testimony shows that even in the United States, the rules governing gender are strictly enforced in everyday life. When identity rules are violated, they can disrupt the normal flow of interaction and produce strong emotional reactions that may even lead to violent confrontations.

Not all identities are as powerful or as dominant as those of gender. Some identities are more or less transitory and temporary (e.g., pregnant, college student); others arise only in particular situations or specific interpersonal relationships (e.g., customer, boyfriend) and many have only weak links to the distribution of scarce resources (e.g., parent, soccer fan). But the identities that are most central to the structure of inequality in modern society, such as those associated with race, gender, social class, and sexual orientation, tend to have a long history of political and cultural conflict. They are recognized across most social situations, they usually stay with us forever, and they will most certainly have a profound impact on our life circumstances, opportunities, and experiences. For all of these reasons, the relationship between identity and inequality involves much more than the straightforward application of a category label.

Inequality is a complex social process through which valued resources are distributed unevenly across individuals, groups, and social categories. Identity is not equivalent to inequality, and it would be naïve to suggest that inequality could somehow be reduced to a game of language or a struggle over the meaning of words. Economic forces, political institutions, cultural traditions, and rules of interpersonal behavior work alongside identity processes to create inequality. To fully understand inequality, we must ask, "How do resources obtain value? What are the social rules for allocating resources? And what are the social processes at work that connect individuals to resources?" Identities are central to answering these questions. All human societies create and use identity categories to explain, justify, and contest the distribution of valued resources. Identity categories define the groups and social categories that receive more or fewer resources. Identity categories are found in the rules used to allocate resources, and identity processes are among the most important mechanisms working to connect individuals to resources.

In this chapter I will begin to explore how identity processes work to elevate the value and power of some persons while diminishing the worth and dignity of others. I start by illustrating important distinctions between *person*, *self*, and *identity*. While these three words are often used interchangeably in everyday language, they are in fact unique sociological concepts. Therefore, to fully understand the relationship between identity and inequality, we must begin with an appreciation of the more fundamental concepts of person and self.

THE PERSON AND HUMAN DIGNITY

Between 1525 and 1866, more than twelve million Africans were hunted, captured, imprisoned, sold into slavery, and shipped to the Americas, where they were forced to labor for the economic benefit of European colonialists and their descendants. Millions died in transit, and millions more suffered debilitating injuries and illnesses. By 1850, there were an estimated four million persons enslaved in the territory of the United States. Of these four million, most were from families who had been in slavery for more than three generations. Slavery was a cornerstone of the American agricultural economy, and it is estimated that by the start of the eighteenth century, about a third of all white households in the United States owned slaves. Imprisoned slaves were considered *chattel* (a piece of property) and subject to being traded, sold, and moved as items of commerce. Between 1790 and 1860, close to one million persons were bought and sold within the borders of the United States, and most of these "transactions" occurred at public markets similar to present-day livestock auctions. Male slaves were called "bucks," and females were known as "breeding winches." A small minority of slaves was allowed to read and write, and a few of these individuals were able to record their experiences in first-person accounts. Below I have reproduced several short excerpts from the written testimony of three slaves.

Testimony of Josiah Henson (1789–1883)[2]
The crowd collected round the stand, the huddling group of negroes, the examination of muscle, teeth, the exhibition of agility, the look of the auctioneer, the agony of my mother—I can shut my eyes and see them all.

My brothers and sisters were bid off first, and one by one, while my mother, paralyzed by grief, held me by the hand. Her turn came, and she was bought by Isaac Riley of Montgomery county. Then I was offered to the assembled purchasers. My mother, half distracted with the thought of parting forever from all her children, pushed through the crowd while the bidding for me was going on, to the spot where Riley was standing. She fell at his feet and clung to his knees, entreating him in tones that a mother only could command to buy her baby as well as herself, and spare to her one, at least, of her little ones. Will it, can it, be believed that this man, thus appealed to, was capable not merely of turning a deaf ear to her supplication, but of disengaging himself from her with such violent blows and kicks as to reduce her to the necessity of creeping out of his reach and mingling the groan of bodily suffering with the sob of a breaking heart? As she crawled away from the brutal man I heard her sob out, "Oh, Lord Jesus, how long, how long shall I suffer this way!" I must have been then between five and six years old. I seem to see and hear my poor weeping mother now.

Testimony of William J. Anderson (1811–?)[3]

In due time we arrived safely in the slave pen at Natchez [Mississippi], and here we joined another large crowd of slaves which were already stationed at this place. Here scenes were witnessed which are too wicked to mention. The slaves are made to shave and wash in greasy pot liquor to make them look sleek and nice; their heads must be combed and their best clothes put on; and when called out to be examined they are to stand in a row—the women and men apart—then they are picked out and taken into a room, and examined. See a large, rough slaveholder take a poor female slave into a room, make her strip, then feel of and examine her as though she were a pig, or a hen, or merchandise. O, how can a poor slave husband or father stand and see his wife, daughters and sons thus treated. I saw there, after men and women had followed each other, then—too shocking to relate—for the sake of money they are sold separately, sometimes two hundred miles apart, although their hopes would be to be sold together. Sometimes their little children are torn from them and sent far away to a distant country, never to see them again. O, such crying and weeping when parting from each other! For this demonstration of natural human affection the slaveholder would apply the lash or paddle upon the naked skin. The former was used less frequently than the latter, for fear of making scars or marks on their backs, which are closely looked for by the buyer. I saw one poor woman dragged off and sold from her tender child—which was nearly white—which the seller would not let go with its mother. Although the master of the mother importuned him a long time to let him have it with its mother, with oaths and curses he refused. It was too hard for the mother to bear; she fainted and was whipped up.

Testimony of Harriet Jacobs (1813–1897)[4]

But I now entered on my fifteenth year—a sad epoch in the life of a slave girl. My master began to whisper foul words in my ear. . . . He tried his utmost to corrupt the pure principles my grandmother had instilled. He peopled my young mind with unclean images, such as only a vile monster could think of. I turned from him with disgust and hatred. But he was my master. I was compelled to live under the same roof with him—where I saw a man forty years my senior daily violating the most sacred commandments of nature. He told me I was his property; that I must be subject to his will in all things. My soul revolted against the mean tyranny. But where could I turn for protection? No matter whether the slave girl be as black as ebony or as fair as her mistress. In either case, there is no shadow of law to protect her from insult, from violence, or even from death; all these are inflicted by fiends who bear the shape of men. The mistress, who ought to protect the helpless victim, has no other feelings towards her but those of jealousy and rage. The degradation, the wrongs, the vices, that grow out of slavery, are more than I can describe. They are greater than you would willingly believe.

These firsthand descriptions of life as a slave paint a horrific picture of brutality, cruelty, and indifference to human suffering. Moreover, we know that the experiences of William J. Anderson, Josiah Henson, and Harriet Jacobs were neither exaggerated nor unique. Torture, rape, and physical confinement were common. The vast majority of white colonists and citizens not only accepted this violent institution, but they promoted it and benefited from it. Slavery was not the work of a few evil leaders who took their followers down a deviant path. It persisted for over three hundred years because it was profitable, legally advanced by politicians, morally justified by religious leaders, and embedded in the habits and practices of everyday life. In other words, slavery was normal, customary, routine, and, for the most part, unquestioned.

How is this possible? How can so many generations of people witness and promote such an appalling and shocking system of inequality? The answer to this question is not simple, and an accurate response depends in large part on the level of analysis one desires. However, when we narrow our focus to the level of interaction, where people are in actual physical proximity with each other, one critical factor stands out: Slaves were dehumanized. For slavery to succeed, slaves had to be defined by the white majority as *inherently* unequal, as a different type of species, and as incomplete persons. Indeed, the historical evidence is unambiguous: White children learned from their parents that black people were inferior, school teachers explained how the "negro race" was physiologically closer to apes, and in churches, white clergy used the Bible to justify white privilege and the submission of slaves.

For this reason, the idea of personhood is key to understanding the ravages of slavery. But dehumanization and depersonalization is a process that is also central to many other forms of inequality. Brutal forms of inequality are not natural to our species. Before the pain and suffering of other human beings can be accepted, justified, and promoted, the victims must have their personhood challenged or denied. We have seen this in the US policy of genocide against indigenous people; it was part of the Nazi Holocaust that targeted Jewish people, homosexuals, and the disabled; and it has historically been associated with violence against women.[5] Thomas Jefferson, the author of the Declaration of Independence, was arguing in support of war with Native Americans when he wrote: "This unfortunate race, whom we had been taking so much pains to save and to civilize, have by their unexpected desertion and ferocious barbarities justified extermination and now await our decision on their fate."[6] Adolf Hitler initiated his justification of the Holocaust by ascribing subhuman characteristics to Jewish people: "The personification of the devil as the symbol of all evil assumes the living shape of the Jew."[7] And the exclusion of women from the rights of citizenship in democracies across the globe was widely justified by arguing that women were in fact "nonpersons" from a legal perspective.[8]

A critique of inequality must, therefore, begin with the assertion that all human beings are persons. Personhood is not a matter of degree or a matter of capacity. One cannot be more or less of a person. Skin color, ethnicity, intelligence, gender, physical ability, or past behavior do not alter or limit personhood. The unconscious, the quadriplegic, the new-born infant, and the infirmed elderly are all full and complete persons. This may seem like an obvious generalization, but it is an assertion that carries with it significant implications. By recognizing the universality of personhood, we are also acknowledging the fact that all humans have dignity. In other words, dignity is an inherent and natural quality of personhood. This is an important point that has been recognized by a diverse group of philosophers, theologians, religious groups, world leaders, and ordinary people.[9]

When the United Nations was formed at the end of the Second World War, the founding charter declared faith "in the dignity and worth of the human person." In a similar manner, the Universal Declaration of Human Rights asserts, "All human beings are born free and equal in dignity and rights." Academic discussions of dignity often begin with reference to Immanuel Kant, the German philosopher whose work at the turn of the eighteenth century is considered a cornerstone of modern philosophy. For Kant, humans must be guided by a "categorical imperative" to act toward each other as an end in itself and never as a means to an end.[10] Which is to say, our humanity requires that we avoid treating each other as objects. This unbreakable relationship of human personhood and dignity is well articulated by sociologist Christian Smith:

> Dignity makes persons innately precious and inviolable. Because of this dignity, human persons are naturally worthy of certain kinds of moral treatment by themselves and in their mutual relations—in particular, of respect, justice, and love. . . . All of this pertains by the virtue of the nature of human personhood, not because the state or "society" says so. If these do say so, it is because they rightly recognize what is objectively true in reality, not because governments or societies have the power by declaration to make it true or untrue.[11]

All human beings are persons, and all persons are innately dignified and worthy of care and just treatment. Nevertheless, the dignity that inheres in humans by virtue of our personhood does not prevent us from ignoring or violating this objective fact. Indeed, in our day-to-day relations with each other we routinely act in small ways that are contrary to the principle of human dignity. When a teacher mocks or embarrasses a student in class, when a student bullies another in the hallway, or when anyone is neglected or ignored, we fail to honor the dignity of persons.

These everyday indignities are hurtful and upsetting, to be sure, but the violation of human dignity is especially disruptive and more egregiously disturbing when it is systematically embedded in the structure of our social institutions. This is why the practice of slavery within the United States, the administrative policies of extermination by Europeans and their descendants that targeted the indigenous peoples of the Americas, and the genocidal assault on Jewish people in Europe by German Nazis were so despicable and appalling. We are offended by these dark moments in our history, not only because they normalized and justified inequality, but also because they represent social configurations that systematically denied dignity to an entire category of people.

The examples of institutionalized inequality from our past highlight the challenge we face in recognizing the social practices, policies, and institutions that restrict personhood and constrain human dignity today. With the advantage of historical perspective our vision tends to improve, and moral boundaries that were once invisible or fuzzy become clear and in focus. For example, it is now obvious to most of us that when women were deprived the right to vote, dignity was denied. When US citizens of Japanese descent were removed from their homes and confined to internment camps during the Second World War, dignity was denied, and when gay and lesbian couples were excluded from certain occupations and legal marriage, dignity was also denied. But what about today? Are there institutions and practices at work in society today where persons are treated as objects and where human dignity is systematically ignored or challenged? Are there experiences in our lives at this moment that will offend future generations?

One possibility may be the organized disregard for human dignity that often occurs in the workplace. To be sure, some of us are fortunate enough to have a job where we experience respect and a sense of self-worth, where we are provided opportunities for professional growth and skill development, where we have the opportunity to be resourceful and creative, where we produce a service or product that fills us with pride, where we have sufficient discretion and control over our work hours, where we feel secure about our future, and where we are fairly and equitably compensated. But for most people in the world today, workplace experiences do *not* come close to achieving these qualities. Most people in the world today have jobs where they are deprived of a living wage, and where they perform repetitive, mind-numbing tasks, are exposed to health and safety risks, and feel objectified, underappreciated, and disrespected.

The struggle for personhood and dignity in the workplace first emerged as an especially salient cause during the so-called Industrial Revolution when machine power transformed the economies of Europe and North America during the late eighteenth and early nineteenth centuries. It was during this period of time that men, women, and children left peasant life, agricultural production, and craft work to labor in the new factories, mines, and mills that sprung up alongside the developing urban centers. This new type of labor was clearly a "means to an end" as opposed to "an end in itself." Workers became objects of production, no different in most cases from the machines that they operated or worked alongside. The labor was long, dirty, dangerous, and exploitative. Typical factory jobs required fourteen-hour days, six days a week, with only an hour or less for rest. Young children were often hired over adults because of their small stature, ease of control, and lower wages. Physical beatings for poor performance were common, and the work was so dangerous that physical deformity and limb amputations were regular outcomes of factory labor. By way of illustration, journalist John Brown describes a gruesome incident that occurred in one British woolen mill in 1828:

> A girl named Mary Richards, who was thought remarkably handsome when she left the workhouse, and, who was not quite ten years of age, attended a drawing frame, below which, and about a foot from the floor, was a horizontal shaft, by which the frames above were turned. It happened one evening, when her apron was caught by the shaft. In an instant the poor girl was drawn by an irresistible force and dashed on the floor. She uttered the most heart-rending shrieks! Blincoe ran towards her, an agonized and helpless beholder of a scene of horror. He saw her whirled round and round with the shaft—he heard the bones of her arms, legs, thighs, etc. successively snap asunder, crushed, seemingly, to atoms, as the machinery whirled her round, and drew tighter and tighter her body within the works, her blood was scattered over the frame and streamed upon the floor, her head appeared dashed to pieces—at last, her mangled body was jammed in so fast, between the shafts and the floor, that the water being low and the wheels off the gear, it stopped the main shaft. When she was extricated, every bone was found broken—her head dreadfully crushed. She was carried off quite lifeless. [12]

While many governments have long since instituted legal reforms concerning the length of the workday, child labor, minimum wages, and workplace safety, the dehumanizing conditions of factory work continue to this day, especially in developing countries where industrial production is expanding. This is because the same economic model that legitimated and justified the dehumanizing conditions of industrial labor two hundred years ago remains in place. It is a model where the realization of profit and the accumulation of capital are taken as an economic necessity and a primary objective. As a consequence, concern for the dignity of workers is usually of secondary importance. In other words, the very structure of the employer-employee relationship is one in which the worker is typically a means to an end as opposed to an end in itself.

THE SELF AS A SOCIAL PROCESS

In the previous section I argued that the concept of personhood is fundamental to understanding inequality. All human beings are persons and all persons have dignity. The inviolable relationship between personhood and dignity is not earned, is not a matter of physical or mental ability, and is not unique to one culture or one historical period. All persons, by virtue of being human, possess an inherent dignity. However, this does not mean that personhood and dignity are always and everywhere recognized and honored. Indeed, our species has a long history of building dehumanizing social structures where personhood is challenged and dignity is denied. Yet at the same time, one of the more unique qualities of our species is that we have the capacity to empathize with others and change our social arrangements when we recognize the harm of our actions. To appreciate this unique capability, we need to understand the self as a social process.

I would like to begin this section with three very brief examples. The three stories are unrelated but they follow a similar path: the commitment of a harmful act, recognition of the indignity of one's behavior, and a public statement of contrition.

Emory University

The white granite buildings of Emory University are nestled within a leafy hardwood forest alongside Candler Lake in a posh neighborhood outside of Atlanta, Georgia. The shaded walkways, cascading water features, and neatly manicured lawns offer a serene environment for the more than thirty thousand students, faculty, and staff who live and work on the pristine campus. But the idyllic Emory campus of today belies a more contentious history. When this prestigious institution was established in 1836 by a small group of devout Methodists, the atmosphere was far from peaceful. The original founders and other early leaders of the new private college were white men who owned slaves, defended the institution of slavery, and used slave labor to build and maintain the campus.

It took almost two centuries, but 175 years after its founding, the Emory University trustees adopted the following resolution in 2011:

> Emory acknowledges its entwinement with the institution of slavery throughout the College's early history. Emory regrets both this undeniable wrong and the University's decades of delay in acknowledging slavery's harmful legacy. As Emory University looks forward, it seeks the wisdom always to discern what is right and the courage to abide by its mission of using knowledge to serve humanity.[13]

Jay Z

Jay Z is one of the most recognizable and successful hip-hop artists in the world. He has sold over seventy-five million records and received nineteen Grammy Awards, and he leads an entertainment and fashion enterprise that has earned him a net worth of more than $500 million. Jay Z advocates for positive social change, and many of his lyrics address the challenges of poverty, crime, and racism. But there is also a less sensitive and more troubling characterization of women that can be found in some of his early work. For example, in *Big Pimpin'*, which was released in 2000, he raps with swagger and bravado about the physical and sexual domination of prostitutes in a lyric laced with demeaning and vulgar references to women.

The song was a commercial success and was ranked on *Rolling Stone*'s 500 Greatest Songs of All Time. But in an interview with the

Wall Street Journal in 2010, Jay Z confessed that he is ashamed of the song and regrets writing the lyric: "It was like, I can't believe I said that. And kept saying it. What kind of animal would say this sort of thing? Reading it is really harsh."

David Blankenhorn

In 2008, the citizens of California passed Proposition 8, also known as the California Marriage Protection Act. The language of the new law was brief and direct: "Only marriage between a man and a woman is valid or recognized in California." Opponents of the proposition challenged the new law as an unconstitutional infringement on the rights of gay and lesbian couples. When the California Supreme Court considered the issue in 2010, one of the most prominent defenders of the new law was David Blankenhorn, an expert witness and founder of the Institute for American Values. In testimony that lasted for more than seven hours, Blankenhorn argued that same-sex marriage harms children, will have negative consequences for society, and should be banned. The Court disagreed and overturned Proposition 8. Two years later, David Blankenhorn changed his mind on gay marriage. In an opinion piece published in the *New York Times*, Blankenhorn explained that he now believes in "the equal dignity of homosexual love" and has come to the realization that "the time for denigrating or stigmatizing same-sex relationships is over. Whatever one's definition of marriage, legally recognizing gay and lesbian couples and their children is a victory for basic fairness." [14]

※ ※ ※

There is nothing special about these three examples. Similar atonements for harmful behavior are familiar, especially from individuals and institutions with highly visible, public reputations. But all three illustrate our uniquely advanced capacity to recognize dehumanizing actions, even in cases where we are the perpetrators. Jay Z acknowledged that his lyrics were devoid of human sensitivity toward women, Blankenhorn recognized that his views disparaged the dignity of homosexual love, and Emory University conceded that its failure to acknowledge the legacy of slavery was inconsistent with its mission to serve humanity.

Our capacity to look back on our past behavior and evaluate how our actions may have harmed others is a powerful skill that is associated with the development of *self*. In sociological theory the concept of self has a distinct meaning that goes beyond our common understanding of the term in ordinary language. For most sociologists, the self is understood to be a dynamic process that grows slowly and requires social interaction for its development. Persons are not born with a self. The self emerges from our social relationships and conforms to the cognitive, emotional, and cultural parameters of the larger society. George Herbert Mead (1863–1931), the American philosopher who is credited with developing and elaborating this particular conceptualization of the self, reasoned that "the whole (society) is prior to the part (individual), not the part to the whole; and the part is explained in terms of the whole, not the whole in terms of the part or parts."[15]

Mead's conceptualization of the self remains influential, and it serves as the foundation for the definition of self that I employ in this book. For Mead, the self is *both* a subject (the acting person) and an object (who we are in society). This means that a fully developed self is, on the one hand, a social force (self as subject) with the capacity for planning, creating, and initiating interaction, and on the other hand, it is also a social product (self as object), which means it is constrained by the rules and structures of the society within which it develops.

These two dimensions of the self operate simultaneously so that socially mature persons are regularly engaged in a process of action and evaluation. We act as a subject and evaluate our self as an object, but the self as an object is also the foundation for the self as subject. Sometimes the self is working to adjust our actions on the fly, while we are in the middle of interacting with other people. In these moments we are socially aware of what we are saying and doing, and we are making immediate adjustments to our behavior. Other times, however, we might have some distance from our past actions as we think more generally about who we are, what we have done, and who we would like to be in the future. Charles Horton Cooley, a contemporary of Mead's, called this the *looking glass self*, because others' reactions to our behavior serve as the mirror that we use to see our own reflection. In other words, we are able to assess our self as an object in society through *perspective-taking*—that is, by taking the perspective of other persons. We are in essence asking ourselves: "How do I appear to be from someone else's point of view?" Here it is important to note that the "others" that we use as our looking glass come in many different shapes and sizes. At times an "other" will be very specific, such as a friend, relative, or teacher. Other times it will be a more "generalized other," such as one's family, church, or society—where many similar points of view come together as an organized whole.

Some commentators have speculated that Jay Z's reassessment of his misogynistic lyrics was an outcome of his marriage to Beyoncé and the birth of their daughter. If so, it may be that Jay Z began to see himself from the perspective of the specific women in his life. David Blankenhorn, on the other hand, had a more generalized reflection and admits that he started to change his mind on gay marriage after the negative public backlash to his court testimony provoked a more heartfelt consideration of gay couples and their families. Finally, the trustees of Emory University were compelled to offer a public statement of regret after hearing from faculty, staff, and students who met in numerous groups over several years to discuss issues of race and ethnicity. The process produced "a new level of understanding of Emory's complex heritage around race and slavery, dating to antebellum days."[16] The collective self-reflection of those affiliated with Emory University is perhaps the most generalized of all in that the offending actions of slavery occurred centuries prior to the apology.

If we are healthy and engaged in regular interaction with others, we will develop a capacity for self-reflection and role-taking. But this is a gradual process that does not occur overnight. It presupposes an ability to understand and use symbols, and for this reason, it roughly corresponds to the development of language. With the use of language and other forms of symbolic interaction (e.g., nonverbal gestures and signs), we are able to stand (symbolically) outside of our own bodies and view the world from other points of view. Infants can't do this, and for this reason, babies appear oblivious to social constraints. It is impossible for a very young child to feel embarrassed or humiliated. Adults can take the role of the infant, but the infant can't yet take the perspective of the adult. Feelings of mortification, humility, pride, and shame are social emotions in the sense that they presuppose a social evaluation of some sort and operate through the self as a social process. Without a fully developed self, life is egocentric, narrow, and inward-looking. As we mature physically and socially, our experience with a more diverse set of others tends to widen. When this happens, we come to realize that our own life experiences, beliefs, values, and resources are not universally shared. The social diversity of our neighborhood and community is gradually revealed, we start to recognize that there are real social differences in the world, and our behavior changes in response to this realization.

Of course, we can't possibly be engaged in role-taking, self-reflection, and self-evaluation at all times. This would be overwhelming, inefficient, and anxiety-inducing. Much of our behavior is in fact routine and automatic. So while the practice of using self-reflection for the purpose of promoting empathy and positive social change is a central process of the self, it is not always an easy habit to develop. Even when our symbolic capacities are fully functional, and we have learned to appreciate social differences, there will still be variation in our tendency or willingness to engage in perspective-taking. To put it simply, some people are less likely to take the role of others, less likely to show empathy, and more likely to ignore other people's feelings. Moreover, these differences are not simply personality traits or individual character flaws; it turns out that perspective-taking is linked to the relative status of one's position in society.

A growing body of empirical evidence indicates that the more power one has, and the more control one has over scarce resources, the less likely one is to consider another person's point of view; or put another way, low-status individuals tend to be better at perspective-taking. This makes logical sense in that power allows for independence; the more power one has, the less concerned one *needs* to be about other people's thoughts and actions. People with less power, on the other hand, have lives that are often controlled by others and will ignore the needs and attitudes of powerful people at their own peril. The employee, for example, must be sensitive to the employer's wishes if he or she wants to stay employed, and students will do better in the classroom when they take the perspective of the teacher.

Because people with less power are more likely to engage in perspective-taking, they tend to do a better job of correctly identifying the attitudes, needs, and interests of other people, and they also tend to have understandings of others that are more complex, sophisticated, and nuanced.[17] Powerful individuals, on the other hand, have a tendency to rely more heavily on social stereotypes in evaluating other persons, and as a result, they tend to be less accurate in their identification of someone else's point of view.[18]

A recent study illustrates the significance of this body of research for understanding inequality. Sociologists Tony Love and Jenny Davis were interested in seeing if they could *manipulate* or change a person's accuracy as a role-taker by simply changing their social status in an artificial experimental setting.[19] Prior research has shown rather consistently that women tend to be more accurate than men when asked to take the perspective of other people. This pattern conforms to traditional gender stereotypes that frame women as being more caring, sensitive, and "in tune" with others. But is this difference "natural," or is it a reflection of the fact that women typically find themselves in less powerful social positions? To answer this question, 160 undergraduate students at an American university were recruited to participate in an experiment. In phase one of the study, the accuracy of each person's role-taking ability was first assessed. As expected, women outperformed men when asked to predict how other people responded to a detailed questionnaire. However, in the second phase of the study, this gender difference disappeared after women were given a high-status supervisory position in a simulated role-playing game. In other words, accuracy as a role-taker had more to do with the status or power of one's social position than gender per se. Of course, this is only one study, but the findings follow a pattern that has been established over a number of years by researchers using a variety of different research methodologies.[20]

Taking the role of other is also significant because it is often a prerequisite for reducing inequality between groups. Most of us are aware that inequality exists, and we recognize the fact that some groups, or categories of people, have access to more resources than other groups of people. But too often our understanding of group differences in power and prestige rests upon prejudicial and discriminatory belief systems that have solidified over time. We might assume, for example, that African Americans are on average less well-off than white people because they are lazy or shiftless, or that women earn less than men because they are too weak and emotional. These false beliefs are often passed from one generation to the next even though they have no basis in fact. But when we are encouraged to consider inequality from the perspective of the poor and the powerless, the evidence shows that calcified prejudices begin to crumble and group conflict dissipates. This does not mean that mutual understanding will by itself eliminate inequality, but more accurate role-taking can reduce barriers that stand in the way of political solutions and the building of community solidarity.

The self is a powerful mechanism for regulating human social behavior. While other animal species have displayed a rudimentary capacity for self-recognition, these skills pale in comparison to the sophisticated symbol-using skills of *Homo sapiens*. We are not born with a self. The ability to take the perspective of the other, evaluate our own actions, and recognize our self as an object in society, develops gradually as we mature both socially and physically. But once this capacity is fully formed, we will be adept at self-reflection and self-evaluation. In ideal social settings, having a mature self will increase our sensitivity to other people's circumstances, and we will be motivated to preserve the dignity that inheres in all persons. But human social interaction is complex, and numerous factors intervene to either limit or enhance this ideal social process. One of the more important intervening variables is identity.

IDENTITY, DIFFERENCE, AND INEQUALITY

In her book *Shades of White*, sociologist Pamela Perry chronicles her experience as a participant observer in two high schools in northern California.[21] For a period covering two academic years she would walk the halls, attend classes, and generally "hang out" with a diverse group of students, male and female, white and nonwhite alike. Over time she built up trust, developed friendships, shared meals, was invited to parties, visited student homes, and conducted lengthy in-depth interviews. Her goal was to capture the authentic voice of students, to witness their interactions and come to an understanding of the different social identities that students used to structure their lives.

High school is a place where social identity becomes particularly salient for young people who are transitioning from adolescence to adulthood. It is a time when novel social identities are often constructed and performed while older and more traditional identities are frequently questioned or rejected. New adolescent identities typically reflect the different social groups, friendships, and cliques that develop in high school, but these quite frequently intersect with other, more dominant and enduring categories associated with race, class, and gender. This is certainly what Perry discovered in her research.

At Valley Groves, a mostly white and middle-class school with about 1,600 students, the largest category distinction in student culture was between "popular" students and students who were not popular. Popular students were also considered "normal" and tended to conform to mainstream adult expectations, had good grades, were "better looking," were involved in sports, and dressed in a conventional youthful style. They were also identified as "jocks," "preppies," or "muffies," in the case of girls. Students that rejected the "normal" identity or could not achieve the "popular" identity were the "hicks," "skaters," "punks," "hippies," "druggies," and "homies." These students were recognized as "other" than normal, and they associated with groups that sometimes engaged in deviant or illicit behavior, such as smoking and drinking.

Twenty miles down the road from Valley Groves sits Clavey High, a school of similar size but where only 12 percent of the student body was white; most students were African Americans (54 percent), followed by Asians (23 percent) and Latinos (8 percent). Many of the identity labels used at Clavey were similar to those used at Valley Groves, but race was the primary basis for social organization at Clavey, which meant that identity distinctions were made *within* categories of black and white. Thus, one of the students at Clavey had the following to say about black students:

> There's the ghetto people, which are more gangster wannabe type of people. There's a richer and upper class of black people who wear clothes from Macy's and hang out with each other. There's the athletes who are all really popular and stand in the middle of the lower lawn. There's the Muslims. You've seen them on the senior lawn at lunch, praying and stuff.[22]

White students, on the other hand, were classified as either "straights," "skaters," "hippies," "ravers," "white rappers," or "punks," while Asian Americans were subdivided into "native," "FOB" (fresh off the boat), "housers," "techno," and "gangsters."

At both high schools, identity categories were distinguished by a range of different symbols or signifiers associated with unique manners of speech, wardrobe, hairstyle, musical tastes, and overall demeanor. For example, Perry describes a female "punk" who was easily classified because she "wore ripped-up, green army fatigue, painted combat boots, and a silver studded dog collar around her neck. She shaved her head close to the scalp with the exception of a strip in the front that spiked out about four inches from her forehead."[23] And a Latina whose family immigrated from El Salvador some years earlier made it clear that students are consciously aware of how different styles are used to mark one's social identity: "For my race, if you start wearing a lot of gold, you're trying to be black. If you're trying to braid your hair, you'll be accused of trying to act black. I'm scared to do things 'cause they might say, 'That's black!' Or if you're Latino and you listen to that, uh, you know, like Green Day . . . then you wanna be white."[24]

The significance of student identity categories is well known to anyone educated in the United States. Indeed, American popular culture is saturated with stories and representations of high school cliques and the relative power, status, and moral worth of different social groups. Too often, however, these stories of identity leave the impression that the grouping and labeling of people end with high school graduation. The truth is, we continue to use social identities in a very similar manner for the rest of our lives. The names and classifications may change, but the same identity processes remain central to almost every type of human social interaction. Perry's research focuses on high school, but it can also be used to illustrate three basic elements that characterize all social identities. I will refer to these as: (1) identity meanings, (2) identity boundaries, and (3) identity negotiations.

Identity Meanings

Every social identity has a shared definition and a common meaning. The *meaning* of an identity can encompass a wide range of cognitive and emotional responses, including expectations for behavior and generalized beliefs, as well as stereotypes and assumptions about value and power. Sometimes the meaning of an identity is widely held across a broad range of people, while other times the meaning may be narrow and only understood within a small group of insiders. Students at Clavey High, for example, understood the difference between someone who was "techno" and someone who was a "houser," but few people outside of this limited social world would likely claim either social identity. And today, if these category labels are still being used, there is a good chance that their meaning has changed. On the other hand, the identities of "white," "black," "student," "teacher," "man," "woman," "gay," and "straight" are more universally understood and widely claimed, and they have meanings that are more enduring.

It may seem somewhat counterintuitive, but the shared meaning of broad-based social identities, such as those that define race, class, and gender, are often more difficult to articulate. This is because widely held identities are often assumed to be "natural" or "normal," and they are not easily recognized as socially constructed identities in the first place. At Valley Groves High, where the vast majority of students was of European descent, all nonwhite racial identities were usually classified as "minorities," and most students struggled when asked to articulate what it meant to be "white." The response of a student named Matt was typical:

> I feel like an American. But I guess I'm kind of jealous because I don't have this kind of ethnic background that I can claim and get college scholarships and stuff. You never see the young white American scholarship foundation, which I think they should have. . . . I guess because the so-called minorities have a lot of ethnic heritage, I don't think white people really have that. Not a strong racial background. They're just kinda there.[25]

Race is without question a dominant identity category in the United States, and the meaning of white versus nonwhite has been used for centuries to enhance the status of some people while challenging the personhood of others. We know, of course, that racial identities have been used historically to segregate schools and to limit the civil rights of some persons while providing greater privilege and opportunity to others. And to this day, all racial identities remain pregnant with meaning, whether we recognize it or not. A person of color who somehow suddenly became white overnight would no doubt experience a very different world as he or she went about daily life. The same is true for white people. A white person who became Asian, black, Latino, or Native American overnight would suddenly experience a very different social landscape premised on the shared cultural understanding of his or her racial category.

There are many different meanings that could potentially be associated with any given identity. Some meanings might be rather neutral and descriptive, as when we associate the identity of "child" with noisy, unpredictable, soft, small, and emotional. For some people, these qualities make children endearing and charming, while for others, these same qualities may be experienced as annoying and bothersome. But most identities evoke meanings that are more clearly positive or negative. The identities of "grandmother," "friend," and "volunteer," for example, have meanings that are almost always highly valued and generally positive, while "sex offender," "neurotic," and "bill collector" are most often devalued and generally negative. In this way, inequality is reflected in the meanings of identities, particularly those identities that are more widely held across society.

Identities defined by categories of race, class, and gender are socially significant because they have historically been used to advantage one class of people over another, and the broad-based meanings of these identities reflect this inequality. Americans of European descent may find it difficult to articulate the meaning of a white racial identity, but most usually admit that white people have traditionally had more value, privilege, and power than other racial identities. We might struggle to define the meaning of rich and poor, upper class and working class, but there is consensus that wealthy people have more value, privilege, and power than poor people. And while the specification of gender differences might be debated, there is no denying that, across the globe, men typically have more value, privilege, and power than women.

This last point should make it clear that identity meanings do not exist independent of real behaviors, physical qualities, attitudes, social relationships, wardrobes, and ways of living. These are the visible differences that make social identities recognizable and real to us. But difference is not the same as inequality. Inequality occurs when more value and power is associated with some identities and not others.

Identity Boundaries

Social identities are not natural. The category labels and meanings that we associate with different types of people are *social constructions*, which means that actual persons had a hand in their creation. When we look at Clavey and Valley Groves high schools, it is easy to see that "jocks," "punks," and "homies" are invented names with constructed meanings attached to persons who share certain qualities. But it is more challenging to believe that *all* identities are similarly invented, even those that are defined by physical differences such as skin color and reproductive organs. We may be born with distinct body parts, hair color, and skin tone, but we are not born with identity labels and meanings attached to these qualities.

Identity boundaries are the symbolic lines that distinguish one type of person from another. Sometimes the boundaries are experienced as fuzzy, flexible, and temporary, while other times the boundaries appear to be clear, solid, and permanent. The category distinctions associated with gender, race, and age employ boundaries that feel relatively concrete because they are based on physical features largely outside of our control. On the other hand, the boundaries that define social class, education, and occupation seem more plastic and flexible because they are rooted in actions and achievements that feel personally manageable and momentary. Language gives us the ability to classify each other into symbolic categories, but there is nothing inevitable about the boundaries that we create to mark one identity category from another.

At Clavey High, students employed flexible boundaries for racial identities that combined both inherited physical characteristics and a distinct behavioral style. This meant that students were consciously aware of their need to perform their racial identity through language, wardrobe, musical tastes, and hairstyle. White student boundaries were marked by standard English, tie-dyed clothing, alternative music, and spiked hair. Asian American identity was symbolized through martial arts, techno music, belled pants, and specific hairstyles that could only be achieved with dense, flat hair. Latino and Chicano identity was defined by Spanish language, traditional Latin music, and high ponytails (for girls). And Black identities were performed by wearing ear studs (for boys), speaking black English, and listening to rap music. By mixing skin color and behavioral style, students would sometimes cross identity boundaries. But when this occurred, students risked being defined as "not black enough," "acting white," or a "wannabe black."

As the above examples suggest, identity boundaries are also significant in the way that they overlap and intersect. All of us claim multiple identities with different meanings that combine to produce a unique social conglomeration. A woman could, for example, be a married, lesbian Latina, a mother with two children, who holds a degree in biology, owns a small business, is a registered Democrat, and belongs to a Catholic parish. One is never just a Catholic, only a woman, or simply a mother. In much the same way that water emerges from the combination of hydrogen and oxygen, intersecting identities will give rise to singularly distinct persons. All of us have an overarching "sense of self" based on an understanding of who we are as a total person. But this very generalized self-image is largely the consequence of the meanings associated with our multiple individual identities. And depending upon the social situation we find ourselves in at any given time, certain identities will be more prominent than others.

When it comes to inequality, the complexity of intersecting identities can make it difficult to sort out the independent effects of bias or discrimination based on categories associated with, say, race, gender, or class. All three of these identity categories are used to sustain inequality, and all three represent categories of people who experience unique forms of injustice and bias. But in high school culture, it appears that class identities are most likely to be obscured.

This is what sociologist Julie Bettie discovered when she conducted her own study of high school identities.[26] Bettie's research strategy was similar to Perry's ethnographic approach, in that Bettie spent an entire year in the hallways and classrooms of a small-town high school in California's central valley. Like Perry, she participated in school events, listened in on student interactions, and conducted in-depth interviews. Although Bettie was primarily focused on female students, her findings were similar to Perry's in that she, too, found student identity groups reflected race and class distinctions that intersected with gender. The "preps," for example, were mostly white, middle-class students taking college preparatory courses, and the "hicks," "smokers," and "trash" were usually poor and white. Mexican American students had their own class-based group identities in the "Mexican preps," "las chicas" and "cholas," where cholas were less settled and considered more "hardcore."

Here, too, different wardrobes, makeup, and hairstyles marked group identities. "Las chicas," for example, wore dark-colored nails, dark lipstick, and tight-fitting pants so as to intentionally distinguish themselves from the more conventional attire of the preps. Social class was, in effect, the most critical identity category for students, but Bettie found that class differences were mostly interpreted by teachers and other adult staff as a reflection of gender and sexuality. In other words, class distinctions were camouflaged by other identities. To quote Bettie: "Class was . . . a present social force in the versions of femininity that the girls performed, but it was unarticulated and rendered invisible because it was interpreted (by school personnel, by preps, and at times by working-class girls themselves) as primarily about gender and a difference of sexual morality between good girls and bad girls."[27] The failure to recognize and articulate social-class identities is not limited to high school youth culture. In the United States, class-based inequalities have persisted since this country's founding, and the gap between rich and poor Americans has been growing larger since at least the 1980s. Still, one's class identity is often concealed or conflated with race, ethnicity, lifestyle, or culture.

Not much is subtle about one's position in the economy. Limited access to wealth, income, job security, and control in the workplace can have an enormous impact on a person's dignity and self-respect. But how does one maintain dignity when unemployed or, when employed, treated like an object or a machine while on the job? How does one garner respect if customers or supervisors are disrespectful? The answer is that workers in modern capitalist economies will often find alternate ways to bolster their sense of worth and competence under challenging economic conditions. One particularly damaging approach involves: (1) constructing identity boundaries between different racial groups, (2) highlighting "moral differences" between groups, and (3) disparaging the characteristics of others. In short, it is a strategy of raising oneself up by tearing others down.

This is well illustrated in Michèle Lamont's classic study of lower-middle class men.[28] Over a period of two years she conducted interviews with working-class men in both the United States and France and found significant differences in the meaning of their class identities. But she also found that white men in both countries established moral boundaries between themselves and "others," where others were typically defined in terms of gender, race, or status as an immigrant. In the United States, for example, one way workers tended to empower themselves was by rejecting economic measures of success in favor of moral standards of self-worth. For white workers, this meant an emphasis on a *disciplined self* with a strong work ethic and a sense of responsibility. For black workers, this meant an emphasis on a *caring self* where morality, solidarity, and generosity are highlighted. As a consequence, even when black and white workers shared the same class identity, they focused on value differences associated with their different racial identities.

We see this in the interviews Lamont conducted. Because white workers emphasized the importance of discipline and responsibility, they had a tendency to see blacks as undisciplined and without a sense of family responsibility. And because black workers placed a greater emphasis on the values of altruism and generosity, blacks had a tendency to see white workers as domineering and cold-hearted. Larry Relles, a police officer in New Jersey interviewed by Lamont, highlights the white moral boundary when he says, "[Blacks] have no sense of family. . . . I come across kids that have no conception of reality, no respect for life, no respect for property, no respect for themselves."[29] And Jerry Flowers, an African American machinist, reinforces a black moral boundary when he tells Lamont, "Black people are sensitive toward human needs because we are concerned humans, whereas the white people that I have met in my life seem detached from the human thing."[30]

These different interpretations of what it means to be black or white not only distract from the common experience of class, but they also reinforce negative racial stereotypes that can lead to uncomfortable and tense interactions between black and white workers. Community solidarity and positive communication require shared meaning, and this is especially true for the meanings associated with dominant social identities. When this does not occur, a process of negotiation over the meaning of each other's identity will often take place.

Identity Negotiations

When Perry was conducting her study of students at Clavey High School, she noticed that racial identity was not entirely determined by skin tone, facial features, or hair type. For the high school students she observed, a person's behavior was also a factor in categorizing someone as black, white, or Latino. Trish, for example, was a student with straight brown hair, blue eyes, and unmistakably pale white skin. However, teachers and students alike would regularly recognize her as black. All of Trish's friends were black, she grew up in a mostly black neighborhood, and over time she had adopted a black-vernacular speaking style and the demeanor characteristic of inner-city black youth. In addition, her wardrobe, hairstyle, and fingernails all conformed to the dominant style adopted by young black girls at Clavey. Trish made it clear, however, that she was not setting out to be black: "A lot of my [black] friends go, 'Oh Trish, you're just black,' and I go 'No, no, no! I don't want to seem like [I'm trying to be black]. . . .' I really don't put that label on myself. But they'll say, 'Oh, Trish is black anyway.'"

Trish's reaction to being categorized as black is similar to Betsy Lucal's response to being categorized as a man. Both women could see that their outward appearance did not conform to others' expectations of what it means to be white (in the case of Trish) or what it means to be a woman (in the case of Betsy). But at the same time, both felt hemmed in by the narrow identity boundaries defining race and gender. Trish was not trying to live as a black person, and Betsy was not trying to live as a man. Both Trish and Betsy were clear that they would rather be accepted for who they are: women who prefer hair, a wardrobe, and a style more common among black girls and men, respectively. Lucal articulated her preference well when she wrote, "I do not want people to see me as genderless as much as I want them to see me as a woman. That is, I would like to expand the category of 'woman' to include people like me."[31]

The experiences of Trish and Betsy are examples of what sociologists call *identity negotiation*. Identity negotiation occurs when people engaged in an interaction attempt to answer two interrelated questions: "Who are you?" and "Who am I?" Most of the time, consensus regarding each other's identity is rather easy to come by and negotiation is unproblematic and unnoticeable. But sometimes the identity we claim is not recognized or accepted. In other words, who we think we are does not match who others think we are. In circumstances where serious negotiation occurs, it will usually take one of two overlapping forms: (1) disagreement over the actual identity that is being claimed or (2) disagreement over the *meaning* of the identity that participants have already agreed upon. The first form tends to be more disruptive and it is often quite embarrassing and emotionally uncomfortable for the participants. The second is typically more subtle and nuanced.

If you claim to be a woman and others categorize you as a man, normal interaction will be blocked until a tentative agreement about your gender identity is negotiated. Strategies for reaching agreement can range from direct confrontation and questioning to more delicate and subtle hints and suggestions. Because identity categories linked to inequality in a society (such as gender and race) are usually central to our overall sense of self (and are used to structure face-to-face interactions), disagreement over these identities will usually be more disruptive. For example, Professor Lucal notes that negotiation over her gender identity will sometimes result in a store clerk demanding that she produce a driver's license to verify her identity as a woman. And while she has learned to anticipate such requests and prefers to negotiate a courteous resolution to the dispute, these moments are fraught with tension and stress on both sides of the interaction.

A more common form of identity negotiation involves disagreement over the *meaning* of already established identities. When a mother and her daughter argue over a curfew time, they have already accepted each other's identity, but they may have very different interpretations of what it means to be a responsible mother and what it means to be a responsible daughter. The mother might still see her daughter as a child, while the daughter sees herself as a young adult. Here, the identities of mother and daughter are not in question, but the meanings of these identities are being contested.

A similar negotiation might occur if a young man were to pay me a visit on campus during my office hours. It is unlikely that the two of us would have a negotiation over my identity as the professor and his identity as the student. At this particular time and place, I would be expecting students to enter my office, and students are expecting to find a professor sitting at a desk. Nevertheless, there is a good chance that the two of us *will* in fact engage in a negotiation over the *meaning* of the young man's student identity. Is he serious, attentive, inquisitive, and responsible? These will usually be the meanings that the student would like to establish. If, however, I have given the student a D+ on a paper, my own interpretation will likely be less positive, and the student will be motivated to change my understanding of his student identity.

It should be rather obvious that most of us are looking to negotiate positive meanings for our identities. We typically want others to see us as "serious student," "nurturing parent," "loving grandmother," "good lover," "honest politician," or "hard worker." But there are exceptions, and sometimes the negotiation of positive identity meanings is not our first priority. In fact there is a solid body of empirical evidence indicating that we are also motivated to maintain *consistency* in our identity meanings—even if this means maintaining an identity meaning that is somewhat negative.[32] I will have more to say about this in the next chapter, but for now it is enough to know that identity negotiation is complicated by the fact that we claim multiple identities that contain multiple meanings and multiple sources of motivation.

Moreover, not all of our identities are equal in their importance; some are more dominant, permanent, and influential than others. When we walk down the street, enter a store, attend a parent-teacher conference, interview for a job, or board an airplane, we will be examined and evaluated in terms of our most visible or socially relevant identities. In these public locations, identities associated with gender, race, class, and age tend to prevail over others—whether we like it or not. In more specific encounters, the situational context may highlight one identity over another, but our socially dominant identities are always in the background, coloring and influencing the perceptions and actions of others. To a hospital administrator one is never just a "patient"; one might also be an elderly female with no health insurance. To a police officer one is never just a "speeder"; one might also be a young, black male driving a late-model automobile. And to a teacher, one is never just a student—one might also be a poor Latino whose parents struggle with English. Although we may desire a world that is identity-blind, this is not a realistic option. Identities matter; they matter to both friends and enemies, to both family and strangers, and they especially matter to the explanation of inequality. In this fact we face an apparent social dilemma: Identities may be used by other people to classify or label us in ways that are not always pleasant or helpful, but at the same time, they provide security and guidance as we use them to establish relationships, build community, and create a meaningful life. In the next section I will take a closer look at the different ways in which socially constructed identities reflect inequality.

IDENTITY MEANINGS AND FORMS OF INEQUALITY

Identity labels have no doubt been employed since the emergence of language itself. When our earliest ancestors first encountered another band of *Homo sapiens* one hundred thousand years ago, they likely created symbolic boundaries to mark and identify each other's family group.[33] But these first identity categories were only used to mark difference; they were not themselves the cause of inequality. It is only when repeated transactions across group boundaries result in the material advantage of one group over another that inequality develops. When one group gains control over scarce resources, it can then use its power to exploit the other group by creating new boundaries, new identities, and new meanings that can serve to reproduce and legitimate inequality.[34]

We may not know the precise historical origin of our own identity categories, or how specific identity meanings developed over time, but we do know that identities are fundamental to human interaction, they help connect individuals to groups, and they are often used as mechanisms of control and exploitation. We also know that identity categories change over time and can have very different meanings depending upon the historical moment, the current social situation, and the individuals who are involved. In this section I start with these assumptions as I consider the various ways in which identity meanings are linked to different forms of inequality. I will begin with a brief review of a study conducted by sociologist Amy Wilkins that looks at the intersection of race, gender, and social class on two college campuses. Wilkins's research is valuable for a number of reasons, but I will use it mostly to illustrate how identity meanings operate on several different levels.

Wilkins conducted in-depth interviews with black students at two predominantly white universities in the United States.[35] She was interested in learning how the young adults experienced the transition from high school to college and how their racial identities may have changed as a result of the transition. Her findings reveal the tentative nature of our identities and the power of social situations. We see this illustrated, for example, in the experience of Sasha, an African American woman who is a senior at a public university in a midwestern state. Sasha was raised in an upper-middle-class family and attended a predominantly white high school where she adopted a middle-class identity and more or less blended in with the other students. In fact, Sasha's racial identity was not important to her as she was growing up, and she did not spend much time thinking about being black until she reached college:

> Since I've been at [college], I've been so much more aware of it
> (race). Almost every day, almost. I never realized my blackness until

I came here. I never hung out with black people until I came here, never heard specific comments, like black people do this, white people do this and you (a black person) don't do this. I never had such encounters with aggressive racism since I've been here: got on the bus with black friends, [and heard] "nigger, get to the back of the bus."[36]

Other black students, who were also raised in affluent white neighborhoods, were similarly shocked by the racial prejudice they encountered in their new college community. Mei, a junior at a college in a western state put it this way:

There's a lot of ignorant white folks up here, too. They just don't understand and they really don't care to. . . . I don't know, I guess people just talk to me like any type of way, and it's just like, "Don't you hear yourself? That's stupid. You can't just say that to people!"[37]

Both Sasha and Mei assumed that their middle-class identities from their white neighborhoods would translate to their new social environment on a college campus. They anticipated a smooth transition and did not expect their race to be a factor in their encounters with other people. They were wrong. While race may not have been a significant identity to *them*, it *was* a significant identity to *others* in their new college communities. As a consequence, both students had to come to a new understanding of what it meant to be female, middle-class, *and black*. In other words, they had to negotiate new identity meanings for their new social location. In the words of Stephanie, an upper-middle-class black student, "When I came to this school, this was where I started noticing the race thing—a lot. Where I totally almost redefined myself."[38]

By definition, the meaning of an identity cannot be exclusively private or subjective; it must be part of a shared community of understanding. This means that the construction of new identity meanings is always a collective project involving a group of people. One does not have the freedom to ignore an identity category if others consider it important. Similarly, when we are negotiating the meaning of a new identity, we are constrained in part by the stories, images, interpretations, beliefs, and expectations already associated with our identity category. We see this, for example, in the middle-class, black women interviewed by Amy Wilkins. Even though many of these college students were not comfortable "speaking their minds," they found themselves cooperating in the redefinition of themselves as strong, independent, outspoken, and confrontational—qualities that partly reflect existing cultural stereotypes of the black woman. While this understanding of what it means to be a black woman can be a source of pride and solidarity among some African Americans, it can also be an uncomfortable style for others who feel constrained by the negative connotations associated with the stereotype. As Janae, a sophomore at a western university, put it, "I slowly but surely became the outcast, that black bitch, you know. . . . And you know it just so happens that because I'm black, I'm the mean black girl."[39]

A helpful metaphor here is to think of identities as a personal wardrobe in which each of us has access to a different set of clothes. The T-shirt that you wear every day is probably very comfortable and it might do a good job of expressing your "style," but it would also be considered inappropriate or too informal in certain settings—such as a wedding or job interview. If a more suitable shirt is not in your closet, you might be forced to scrounge something from a friend or a family member. But even if you attempt to fashion the borrowed shirt to fit your unique style, there is still a good chance that it will be ill-fitting and feel uncomfortable.

Each of us has access to a wardrobe of identities, and each of us has a measure of control over the identities that we "choose to wear." However, we don't have complete control over the clothes that end up in our closet, the creation of rules for appropriate dress, or the social situations that we find ourselves in. In other words, we have some room to maneuver in the construction of new identity meanings, but we are at the same time constrained by social circumstances and cultural stereotypes outside of our control.

As the examples above suggest, identity meanings "exist" and "operate" at several different layers or levels of analysis. The assumption that black women are outspoken, independent, and strong is an example of an identity meaning at the *level of culture*. Meanings at the level of culture are widely recognized, usually unsophisticated, and they very often reflect well-known stereotypes. Nevertheless, when meeting someone for the first time we usually rely upon these generalized cultural meanings. In this sense, cultural stereotypes are like a skeleton, and subsequent interactions and negotiations add meat to the identity bones.

It is at the *level of interaction* where we are provided an opportunity to negotiate more specific and elaborate identity meanings. When the middle-class black women entered college, they were forced to negotiate new meanings during encounters with others who often relied exclusively on stereotypes. Identity at the level of interaction is therefore an outcome of the immediate social situation. It may incorporate cultural meanings, but it will also be more sophisticated and more elaborate. Most of us resist the meanings associated with cultural stereotypes and prefer to be recognized for who we *really* are. Janae did not want to be known as "the mean black girl" and she was frustrated that she "slowly but surely became . . . that black bitch." We can assume that Janae preferred to be known for her "true" identity meanings, even though she was not always finding success in her negotiations at the level of interaction.

When we are negotiating our identity meanings, we are usually working to move *others'* interpretation of us toward what we believe to be more authentic or ideal meanings. These more "accurate" identity meanings are the meanings that reside at *the level of the person.* Identity at the person level should not be confused with one's personality or character. Personal identity is stitched together from our social experiences and incorporates meanings from both the cultural level and the level of interaction. Identity meanings at the person level are especially critical because it is the place where enduring consequences of inequality are inscribed and scarred onto actual bodies and minds. When Stephanie said, "I totally almost redefined myself," she was articulating the fact that cultural meanings and situational encounters with others changed her *personal* identity meanings.

In the next section I will explore each of these levels of analysis in more depth with particular attention to the way in which inequality is experienced, and uniquely expressed, at the level of culture, the level of interaction, and the level of the person.

IDENTITY MEANINGS AT THE LEVEL OF CULTURE

The government of Mexico does not collect data on race. The Mexican national census does not include questions about race, and many prominent intellectuals contend that racism does not exist in Mexico. Moreover, in Mexican culture, conversations about race or any attempt to classify someone based on race is itself considered racist and personally offensive. When sociologist Christina Sue initiated her study of race in Mexico, she found that the very mention of the word *race* would evoke the idea of racism: "When I asked Javier about his racial identification, he replied 'Mm. Well, I am not a racist. I don't like to be racist. I see the whole world the same, everyone, *morenos* (brown), blacks, whites, I see them all the same.'"[40]

Professor Sue conducted her research in the state of Veracruz, which runs along the gulf coast of Mexico and was the primary port for the African slave trade. As a consequence, Veracruz has a high proportion of residents with African ancestry, as well as black immigrants from Cuba and other Caribbean nations. But the vast majority of residents in Veracruz are considered *mestizo,* which is traditionally defined as a mix of Spanish and indigenous people. The *mestizaje* ideology in Mexico is one that embraces mixed-race people, it is reflected in national symbols and imagery, and it has historically been a guide for public policy. To be mestizo is to be quintessentially Mexican.

The invisibility of traditional racial identities in Mexican culture does not mean, however, that skin color and ancestry are unrelated to inequality. One obvious legacy of Mexico's colonial history is that individuals with light skin and European features are overly represented among the social and economic elites, while the poorest of the poor are overwhelmingly dark-skinned. Veracruzanos may be uncomfortable talking about race and racial identity, but they have no problem using skin color as a descriptor in everyday conversations. Sometimes skin tone is referenced without evaluation, in a manner equivalent to hair color or height. But there are also times when the color of one's skin becomes code for certain implied values linked to race. Sue offers the following example:

> When engaging in conversations about whites, they often supplant the term white with a class term (e.g., "people with money") or an aesthetic referent (e.g., "beautiful people") without explanation . . .

in the Veracruz mind, a conversation about whites is also a conversation about the rich, the powerful, and the beautiful.[41]

Race is also hidden in colloquial expressions such as "having good presentation" and "having good appearance." It is not uncommon for job
advertisements to include a requirement of "good appearance," especially for positions involving customer relations in public places. The
shared understanding in Veracruz is that a "good presentation" means
being well-groomed *and* having straight hair and light skin.

Even though a white European phenotype is clearly associated with
wealth and beauty, Mexicans are typically hesitant to identify themselves as white. Sue and other scholars who have studied race in Latin
America attribute this reluctance to the *mestizaje* ideology, where racial
assimilation is highly valued. The white Spanish colonizers controlled,
exploited, and dominated both dark-skinned indigenous people and
black African slaves, and the legacy of this history is still evident in the
social structure of Mexico. To avoid being perceived as superior or un-
Mexican, persons with European features will readily assert a mestizo
heritage, no matter how thin, so as to intentionally distance themselves
from their Spanish ancestors.

If you are like me, born, raised, and educated in the United States,
the Mexican cultural understanding of race and racial identities might
seem strange. This is because Mexico's unique language, colonial history, indigenous population, and experience with slavery have given rise
to a distinctive set of identity categories that do not "make sense" to
many of us who live outside of Latin America. The Mexican experience
with race illustrates not only how identity categories can vary across
cultures, but it also shows how inequality will persist under different
forms, using different names, and with different symbolic boundaries.
While the Mexican government and people might advance a *mestizaje*
ideology and argue that their country is free of racism, the evidence
suggests a more nuanced story. White skin color and physical features
linked to a European ancestry are privileged in Veracruz and other
regions of Mexico, while at the same time, dark skin, indigenous ancestry, and African features are less highly valued. In other words, while
national borders and cultural traditions may give rise to different identity categories, these symbolic boundaries cannot confine the widespread practice of dominance, control, and exploitation. So while social

identities in different regions of the globe will have different names and will categorize different groups of people, well-worn cultural hierarchies of value and power will persist nevertheless.

The *meaning* of a particular identity usually includes a rather complex expression of overlapping sentiments, behavioral expectations, beliefs, attitudes, stereotypes, and assumptions about a specific class of people, and this elaborate compilation of symbols and boundaries will reflect unique cultural representations. But beneath this intricate exterior, social scientists have uncovered a few basic *dimensions of meaning* that form the core of all identities, irrespective of culture and social structure. An extensive body of research has found that the two most important aspects of meaning are centered on expressions of *value* and *power*—qualities that define inequality. This important discovery was facilitated by the invention of an innovative research tool called the *semantic differential.*

The semantic differential was developed and tested by psychologist Charles Osgood and his colleagues in a series of research papers published in the 1940s and 1950s, and their work was later summarized and elaborated in what is now recognized as one of the most influential books of the era: *The Measurement of Meaning.* [42] In this book, Osgood and his associates focused on the possibility that the affective meanings associated with different persons, objects, and events could be reduced to a small number of *dimensions,* and that these basic dimensions would be the same across all language groups. His initial investigation of anthropological field notes from five widely separated cultures was promising in that he found a striking similarity in word associations. For example, "good" things were regularly associated with "up," "light," "white," "purity," "warm," "dry" and "happy"; while "bad" was regularly associated with "down," "dark," "black," "wet," "cold" and "sad." Building on this initial insight, Osgood then devised a measurement strategy in which cultural stereotypes held toward a particular identity category could be assessed against a pair of opposite adjectives. An example of a sample questionnaire item is presented below:

MEXICANS

kind :_____:_____:_____:_____:_____:_____: cruel

weak :_____:_____:_____:_____:_____:_____: strong

fast :_____:_____:_____:_____:_____:_____: slow

When respondents place a mark closer to either end of the scale they are indicating stronger sentiments toward Mexicans, and the favored adjective is said to represent one element of meaning associated with a "Mexican" identity. After a much longer version of this test was administered to a very large sample using many different adjective pairs, Osgood used what was at the time a relatively new statistical technique known as *factor analysis* to see if there were any clusters of intercorrelations among the adjectives. The results of the first analyses were groundbreaking. Osgood and his research team found that three clusters of adjectives consistently accounted for almost all the differences in meaning. He named these three basic dimensions: *evaluation*, *potency*, and *activity*.

The *evaluation* dimension consisted of adjective pairs that connoted positive or negative value, such as good-bad, nice-awful, sweet-sour, affectionate-hateful. The *potency* dimension included adjective pairs that connoted relative power, such as: big-little, strong-weak, heavy-light, powerful-powerless. And the *activity* dimension referenced movement and action, as in: fast-slow, noisy-quiet, young-old, dead-alive. Over the past six decades, hundreds of studies have replicated Osgood's work across more than twenty different language communities and in dozens of different societies, giving credence to the validity and reliability of the semantic differential as a measurement strategy. Today, the semantic differential is a standard tool for the assessment of identity meanings, and there is wide recognition that representations of value and power are the two most fundamental dimensions of meaning.

The significance of *value* and *power* as the two most important dimensions of meaning cannot be overstated. Not only are these two concepts central to sociological analyses of inequality, but they are also recognized as elemental in numerous other research traditions, including cross-cultural psychology, small-group behavior, and the study of personality and emotion. Psychologists Harry Triandis and his colleagues went so far as to argue that qualities equivalent to value and power are "the fundamental dimensions of human social behavior," a conclusion they reached after an extensive review of the literature that included their own cross-cultural research on family roles, task roles, and interpersonal attitudes.[43] Sociologists Theodore Kemper and Randall Collins concurred but went one step further. After they reviewed findings from a large body of cross-disciplinary research, they concluded that not only are status (value) and power the two most central dimensions of face-to-face interaction, but that they are the cornerstones upon which larger social structures are constructed.[44]

Given the central role of value and power in human social life, it should not be surprising to find that these two dimensions of meaning are also crucial to understanding our identities. At the level of culture, the value of an identity is reflected in differing amounts of respect, prestige, status, and honor, while the power of an identity is defined by variation in control, influence, and authority. Consider, for example, how value and power are evident in various occupational identities. When evaluated in the abstract, we find that "teacher" and "firefighter" receive relatively high ratings in surveys of occupational prestige. In general, Americans respect teachers and believe firefighters deserve to be honored. In fact, "teacher" and "firefighter" are given more honor and respect than either "banker" or "politician." At the same time, however, "banker" and "politician" are, under most conditions, considered more influential and controlling, which is to say they are viewed as more powerful. Again, it is important to keep in mind here that identity categories and identity meanings at the level of culture have a certain degree of independence from actual persons. This is why we can imagine what it would be like to be a "teacher" or a "firefighter" without actually enacting either identity, and it is also why we have no trouble accepting the fact that the third grade teacher at our local elementary school or the captain of our neighborhood fire station will both still "exist" in their respective institutions even after the current teacher and captain retire and their positions are vacated.

Because the value and power of an identity category is widely recognized and understood at the level of culture, it affects the preferences and motivations of individuals who aspire to achieve a certain level of respect and dignity. Most of us desire identities that are highly valued and powerful, and we want to avoid being classified with identities that are disrespected and weak. As such, we find a customary preference for baby boys over baby girls in cultures with a patriarchal family structure. When men have more power and value in a society, the absence of a male heir can result in economic instability and feelings of loss and shame. In China's rural villages, for example, there is a common expression: "The birth of a boy is welcomed with shouts of joy and firecrackers, but when a girl is born, the neighbors say nothing."[45] In most cases, the devaluation of girls has less to do with the actual qualities that women might have in common, and more to do with the fact that they are simply not boys.

But even in modern societies where more egalitarian gender relations have been codified into law and gender preferences for infants have all but disappeared, we still find a persistent cultural favoritism for boys over girls. We see this, for example, in the way parents react when their child's behavior does not conform to traditional gender stereotypes. Little boys who engage in actions that are defined as "obviously feminine" (playing with a Barbie doll, using fingernail polish, wearing "girls' clothes") are more likely to be discouraged by their parents than are little girls who indicate a preference for actions that are defined as stereotypically masculine (playing with trucks, watching football, wearing "boys' clothes").

Research by Emily Kane suggests that this difference reflects both a devaluation of a feminine identity and a fear on the part of parents that their little boys will be shunned and teased if they display traits and behaviors that are seen as stereotypically feminine.[46] As a consequence, even in circumstances where parents profess an egalitarian attitude and proclaim a desire to erase gender stereotypes, there are limits to the promotion of cross-gender behavior. In the words of the mother of a young boy interviewed by Professor Kane: "I would worry if he had too many feminine characteristics, that would worry me. I just want him to be a boy and play with the boys, not to like girl things. If he did that, the boys would think he's weird, and then he'd be lonely."[47] Few parents want their children to be on the battle line of gender equality, and this mother's sincere and candid expression of concern for her son's welfare illustrates that not only is she aware of the larger cultural meanings associated with gender identities, but she is also sensitive to the power and value of these meanings at the level of interaction where her son's safety and dignity rests in the balance.[48]

IDENTITY MEANINGS AT THE LEVEL OF INTERACTION

When we use identities at the level of interaction, we express and embody cultural meanings in our social behavior. Thus, the *value* of an identity is experienced in terms of the relative amount of deference or respect granted to someone in a face-to-face encounter. The *power* of an identity, on the other hand, is realized when the cultural meaning of an identity enhances someone's ability to exert dominance and control. Sometimes we can be rather calculated and strategic as we self-consciously manipulate identity meanings for personal advantage. Other times we experience privilege or impudence without even recognizing that it is attached to an identity category. But under both conditions, the outcome is the same: Identity meanings contribute to the formation of asymmetrical relationships. Persons who hold the less powerful and less valued identity are expected to produce an interactive demeanor that is obsequious, reverential, and submissive, while those who can lay claim to a more highly valued and powerful identity can anticipate more attention, admiration, and influence.

Our capacity to recognize the relative power and value of an identity develops at a surprisingly early age, and there is evidence that children as young as three can be quite proficient at using identity categories to demean and dominate their peers. We see this, for example, in research conducted by sociologists Debra Van Ausdale and Joe Feagin, who followed fifty-eight preschool children for over a year and documented their playground interactions, classroom conversations, and intimate communication with parents, teachers, and friends.[49] To the surprise of most adults, these children were already adept at recognizing racial categories, and some were shockingly effective at using racist language to exclude and hurt other children. The following incidents are only a few of the examples documented by Van Ausdale and Feagin:

- Renee, a white four-year-old, is struggling to pull Lingmai (Asian) and Jocelyn (white) in a wagon across the playground when she suddenly stops, drops the wagon handle, and stands still while breathing heavily. Three-year-old Lingmai then jumps out of the wagon and grabs the handle in an obvious attempt to assist Renee. But Renee refuses the offer, puts her hands on her hips, and admonishes Lingmai: "No, no. You can't pull this wagon. Only white Americans can pull this wagon." Lingmai ignores the command and attempts once again to pull the wagon. But Renee insists for a second time that only "white Americans" are allowed to pull the wagon.

- A daycare worker is pushing children on a tire swing when Felicia, a white three-year-old, objects to an attempt by Joseph (age three and African American) to get a ride on the swing: "Black people are not allowed on the swing right now, especially black boys." Joseph frowns and starts to cry before seeking adult intervention.
- Three-year-olds Brittany (white) and Taleshia (black) are playing in a sandbox when Brittany picks up a rabbit pellet from the sand, holds it next to Taleshia's arm and says, "You're the same color as the rabbit poop." Taleshia frowns while Brittany proclaims, "Your skin is shitty!" and "You have to leave. We don't allow shit in the sandbox."

In each of these examples, the young children demonstrate both knowledge of racial categories and a rudimentary understanding that some racial identities have more value and power than others. But even more surprising is the manner in which these preschoolers have already learned how to use the value and power of identity meanings to advance their interests in playful interactions. Renee, Felicia, and Brittany all show that they are capable of intentionally asserting the privilege and power of their white identity over Lingmai, Joseph, and Taleshia—playmates who are clearly recognized as "nonwhite."

How is this possible? How do preschoolers become proficient at using racial identities to harm and exclude others? There is no doubt that children learn a good deal about race and racial hierarchies from adults. Sometimes kids are simply imitating or modeling the exact words and actions of their parents, and other times they discover identity meanings from books, television, and film. But quite often adults will signal identity meanings to children with very subtle expressions of deference and control that are furtively embedded in the structure of an otherwise ordinary interaction sequence.

One study, for example, analyzed 322 different encounters between pediatricians and their young patients and found evidence of an implicit bias in the way in which the doctors communicated with parent and child.[50] As one might expect, doctors were found to spend more time interviewing parents about the child's illness than they did actually interviewing the child. This is reasonable, since we assume that parents are more knowledgeable and skilled at communication than their children. However, a more surprising and harmful finding from the same study is that physicians were also much more likely to marginalize children if they were from black or Latino families. This was true even when the child's age and the educational background of the parents were taken into account. White children from middle-class families received more direct questions from the physicians, and poor black and Latino kids were more likely to be ignored. In other words, children with devalued identities were disempowered because they were perceived as incompetent. The evidence from this study shows how a seemingly innocuous conversation can serve as a lesson in identity privilege and dominance. When similar interactions occur many times over, children gradually discover the relative value and power of their identity categories.

Still, we must also recognize that children are not simply machines waiting to be programmed. In addition to being very quick learners, children are also teachers. In the Van Ausdale and Feagin preschool study, for example, children were actively probing and cultivating identity meanings in their interactions with each other. Children interact with their peers in a social world that is mostly unnoticed by adults, and so-called kids' culture was also largely ignored in research by an earlier generation of social scientists. Nevertheless, we now know that children make a rather significant and independent contribution to the production of identity meanings at the level of interaction. When kids are at play, they are not merely mimicking adults; they are also testing the boundaries of authority, experimenting with interpersonal power, discovering the significance of their identity categories, and creating new understandings of self.

By the time we reach adulthood, most of us have become experts at using identity at the level of interaction. With years of social experience behind us, we understand the value and power of cultural meanings associated with race, gender, economic class, and sexual orientation, and we are adept at navigating our way through situations that might diminish our experience of worth and dignity. Persons with identities that are culturally devalued are especially skilled at managing identity at the level of interaction. This is because they are more likely to experience the negative emotions of a disruptive and demeaning encounter and must prepare for such an event. As a white, heterosexual male who works on a university campus, I rarely face challenges to my worth and value during my day-to-day interactions with students and staff. When I enter a classroom, my authority is not disputed, my expertise or knowledge is not questioned, and I am generally treated with deference and respect. On the other hand, my colleagues who are *not* white, *not* male, or *not* heterosexual do not experience the same degree of privilege.

One might assume that in a university classroom, the value and power of a "college professor" identity would supersede any stereotypes associated with race and gender. However, a study conducted by sociologist Roxanna Harlow shows that, in fact, black and female faculty members are more likely to find themselves in situations where students question their credibility.[51] For example, one professor (an African American woman) recounted the time when a student refused to believe the veracity of the documented lecture material, challenged the professor in a face-to-face encounter, and then made a point to fact-check the information with other faculty in the department. Another black professor (male) shared a similar story of a white student who was equally incredulous:

> He went so far as to say, when I was trying to explain something, "that's wrong, that's just wrong, that's not true." . . . This is very, very difficult because at the same time, you can't go off on him because you've got to be respectful and you've got to be this professional person and stuff, but it's very, very hurtful, you know, particularly from someone who was not an excellent student.[52]

Recognizing that their authoritative status as a professor cannot be assumed or taken for granted in the classroom, professors with devalued identities have learned to employ certain interactive strategies to bolster their credibility. This might include reviewing one's academic credentials at the start of the term, projecting a strict or authoritative demeanor, and reminding students to call them "Doctor" or "Professor." While it is true that white male faculty members will also use these same tactics from time to time, they are much less likely to do so—mostly because they do not find it necessary. In fact, Professor Harlow's study found that some white male professors actually downplayed their formal academic status so as to appear more approachable to students. As one study participant put it, he likes to include "a certain element of calculated self-deprecation" in his lectures so that students will find him accessible.[53]

Identity negotiations at the level of interaction are at times analogous to hand-to-hand combat where the value and power of our identity categories function as both offensive weapons and defensive armor. With sufficient protection, we have the luxury of remaining oblivious to the challenges of an opponent. But if our "status shield"[54] is weak, our devalued identities make us vulnerable to the slights, insults, and abusive insolence of an adversary. Over the course of our life, successive interactive conflicts can result in wounds that accumulate and scar our sense of self. While these public injuries may feel private and petty, they often produce effects that are profoundly consequential and visible at the level of the person.

IDENTITY MEANINGS AT THE PERSON LEVEL

We use identity categories every day to make sense of our social surroundings, to define and classify other people, and to establish meaning and purpose in our own life. Without the ability to recognize and use identity labels, we would feel confused, lost, and disoriented in a world without structure. In other words, identity categories enable social engagement and are necessary tools for creating community and establishing group solidarity. But at the same time, identities also limit our private actions and restrict our social behavior. We are only free to be the person that our community allows. This is because our freedom to be who we want to be is constrained by the available pool of culturally acceptable identity categories. For example, if I were to claim an identity that is not considered culturally legitimate (e.g., King of America, or God), I risk being ridiculed and ostracized. And if I were to insist on using the same illegitimate identities in everyday interactions, I could end up being forcefully hospitalized or even incarcerated. In the end, our desires and choices usually conform to what is socially acceptable.

Still, identity categories do not make us into rule-following robots, because agency, creativity, and free will are very much a part of the human experience. In fact, without the structure of identity categories, our capacity to communicate would be hampered, and our ability to create and innovate would be stunted. But at the same time, identity categories enable our agency under rather limiting conditions. Although this may seem like an illogical or contradictory statement, resources that enhance our freedom always come with constraints. By way of analogy, think of how an automobile enhances our freedom to travel at a high speed for long distances, while at the same time our journey is necessarily restricted to the places accessible by roads and bridges. In a similar manner, the shared meaning of culturally accessible identities can shape our understanding of self and other in a way that will both enable and constrain our behavior in social situations. This is well illustrated in a classic experiment first conducted by social psychologists Claude Steele and Joshua Aronson.[55]

Steele and Aronson wanted to know if the cultural stereotypes associated with an African American identity could help explain differences in student performance on standardized tests. They designed an experiment that began with black and white college students completing a half-hour test composed of questions taken from the Graduate Record Exam. Under one experimental condition, the students were told that the test was a measure of "verbal reasoning ability" and could be used to assess an individual's "strengths and weaknesses." In a second experimental condition, no reference to verbal ability was made and the students were led to believe that the study was simply looking at "psychological factors involved in solving verbal problems."

While these differences in instruction between the two experimental conditions might appear rather innocuous, they resulted in considerable differences in test performance. When students thought the test was unrelated to verbal ability, there were no differences in test scores between black and white students. But when students believed that their verbal ability was being measured, the African American students performed significantly less well than the white students. According to Steele and Aronson, this finding demonstrates the subtle, but undeniable power of identity stereotypes. When the negative stereotype of blacks as intellectually inferior is made socially salient, black students become anxious, they feel the pressure of a threatening set of cultural meanings, and their test-taking performance is hindered. And because white student identity is not associated with the same negative stereotypes, they do not feel the same pressure or experience the same level of personal anxiety.

Similar findings have been found for numerous other groups with different cultural stereotypes and under different social situations. One study, for example, examined the gender stereotype that men are inherently superior to women when it comes to mathematic ability. In this experiment, researchers found that when students were led to believe that men often outperformed women on a rather difficult math test (stereotype made salient), female students did substantially worse on the test than the male students. But when students were told that the same math test was unrelated to gender (stereotype minimized), gender differences in test performance were eliminated.[56] Another study showed that in certain situations, negative cultural stereotypes could also interfere with athletic success for *both* blacks and whites. When black college students were led to believe that performance on a golf skills task was related to "sports intelligence" (stereotype made salient) they did significantly worse than the white students. But when white students were told that the same golf skills were associated with "natural athletic ability" (stereotype made salient), their performance was significantly worse than that of the black students.[57]

Taken together, this body of research shows that the cultural meanings and generalized beliefs associated with an identity can both enhance and restrict social behavior; one person's freedom can be another person's confinement. When the value and power of an identity category becomes part of a person's understanding of self, we can say that inequality has been internalized. If we happen to internalize identity meanings that are culturally devalued and relatively powerless, we are at risk of psychological harm, and if the material consequences of devalued identities restrict access to education, employment, health care, and a safe environment, we are also at risk of physical harm. Either way, the empirical evidence is clear: Identity meanings have an impact on both mental and physical health.

Most research on the link between identity and mental health has focused on the related concepts of *self-esteem* and *self-efficacy*—personal assessments that are linked to the relative value and power of identities. In this body of work, self-esteem is typically defined as a judgment about one's overall worth, merit, or value. Individuals with negative self-evaluations are said to "have" low self-esteem or a poor self-image. Self-efficacy on the other hand, is conceptualized as a personal assessment of one's level of competence, effectiveness, control, and agency. When self-efficacy is low, individuals tend to have little faith in their ability to successfully complete an action or manage their future. Although psychologists who study self-esteem and self-efficacy tend not to focus their attention on the power of social forces, there is little doubt that negative identity meanings at the level of culture, and degrading or insulting experiences at the level of interaction, can have profound consequences for how one thinks and feels about oneself.

Consider, for example, the personal and social significance of one's social-class identity. Whether we are employed or unemployed, and, if we are employed, the relative amount of authority or control we have in the workplace together with the amount of salary and benefits we receive, have obvious implications for how we see ourselves, how we see others, and how others see us. If we happen to own a profitable business or enjoy a successful career in a respected profession, we will be financially secure, reap the material benefits of a high income, and feel a sense of pride and honor in our achievements. If, on the other hand, our work experience involves menial tasks, a low wage, insecure and short-term employment with little authority, our dignity will be challenged and we will struggle to maintain positive self-esteem and self-efficacy. In this way, the powerful economic and political forces that operate to control opportunities in the labor market can also have definite consequences for the self.

This is well illustrated in sociologist Jennifer Silva's study of working-class young people who entered adulthood at the turn of the twenty-first century under punishing economic conditions.[58] With growing class inequality, declining opportunities for steady employment, mounting debt, and poverty-level wages, the young adults interviewed by Silva had few pathways for security and success, and most were coming up short in their attempt to establish stable relationships. In Silva's assessment, self-esteem and self-efficacy were threatened because "traditional markers of adulthood have been swept away by a rising tide of economic insecurity and social uncertainty that have transformed coming of age into a precarious journey with no clear destination in sight."[59] As a result, she found a growing unease among many young adults who were struggling with issues of identity while questioning their sense of worth and value.

We see this, for example, in the experience of Monica, a thirty-one-year-old art student who dreams of becoming a professional photographer. Monica grew up on a family dairy farm that teetered on the edge of poverty. After graduating from high school, she secured a succession of factory jobs but was laid off from each when the plants were closed.

For the next decade, Monica would repeat a similar pattern of intermittent employment as a waitress, truck driver, farm laborer, telemarketer, and hospital aide before eventually moving back home with her parents to help with the family business. By the age of thirty, Monica had suffered through the dissolution of several personal relationships, had developed a dependency on drugs and alcohol, and was diagnosed with depression. Still, she held out hope for a more stable and promising future, and at the time of the interview she was attending Alcoholics Anonymous meetings, was enrolled in college, and had taken out nearly $30,000 in loans to help pay for tuition and expenses.

It is impossible to know for certain if the unsettled economic circumstances of Monica's life jeopardized her physical and mental health—there are obviously many details that must be taken into account—but the more general relationship between social class, psychological well-being, and overall health is undeniable. The evidence shows quite clearly that poverty and economic instability early in life can set into motion a series of cascading events that increase the prevalence of risky behaviors, family conflict, divorce, disease, and even death.[60] The wounds to the body are often visible and apparent, but harm to "the spirit" is more easily concealed. These are the "hidden injuries of class" that assault a person's dignity, diminish self-respect, and destroy confidence and feelings of control over one's life.[61]

Identity categories are a necessary and essential component of social interaction. Indeed, the use of symbols to categorize and classify the social world is one of the most distinctive features of what it means to be human. It is with the use of identity categories that we come to know self, come to know and understand each other, and come together to build communities of solidarity. And identity is also a source of motivation and aspiration. When we strive for a promising career, work toward an advanced degree, dream about a future marriage, or anticipate life as a mother or father, we employ identity categories to visualize, guide, and construct a possible self with value and dignity. In these instances, we experience identity as a resource for individuality, creativity, and freedom.

Nevertheless, we do not have complete control over the structure and meaning of our identities. This is because the identity categories that we draw upon to construct a meaningful self exist independent of our own unique life. In most cases, identity meanings have emerged from multiple practices of power, conflict, cooperation, and solidarity that preceded our birth. The cultural meanings of our shared identity classifications often feel natural and permanent because we did not witness the long history of turmoil and negotiation that has since settled over time. Our skin color, our body parts, the way we live our life, and the work that we do have already been interpreted for us. We may have some success in negotiating new meanings in our encounters with other people, but the cultural meanings that we inherit are difficult to alter; despite our best efforts, the social expectations of others continue to direct, limit, and control our day-to-day interactions, as well as our personal interpretations of self. This is the irony of the sociological self: Identity categories are at the same time both a resource for freedom and individuality and a source of control and domination. In the words of sociologists Richard Sennet and Jonathan Cobb, "the tools of freedom become the sources of indignity."[62]

SUMMARY

I began this chapter arguing for the inviolable relationship between human personhood and dignity. We are all born full and complete human persons. Personhood is not negotiable. Legal decisions, military interventions, and egregious historical practices have been used over-time to dehumanize, torture, and kill many different categories of people. But even the most abhorrent and despicable acts of mass murder cannot strip away natural personhood. When we recognize the universality of personhood, we are also accepting the fact that all humans have dignity. In other words, dignity is an inherent and natural quality of personhood. Once we acknowledge and accept this principle, we have the moral and ethical foundation for rejecting most forms of inequality.

Although we are all born fully human with inherent dignity, we are not born with the power to communicate with symbols. As a result, infants and very young children cannot see themselves as an object in relation to others, they cannot take the perspective of other people in their lives, and they are unable to engage in self-reflection. These are skills that emerge from human interaction and reflect a level of physical and social maturity not present at birth. But once the self is fully formed, humans display a unique capacity for altruism and an exceptional sensitivity to the plight of others. Under ideal social circumstances, when these exclusively human capacities emerge, we will be motivated to understand each other's point of view, we will begin to recognize each other's humanity, and we will endeavor to preserve the dignity that inheres in each of us.

While it is true that dignity is inherent in all human persons, and all persons have a natural capacity for self-reflection and perspective-taking, identities themselves are neither natural nor universal. Identities are social constructions. We are not born with identities. Identities emerge from specific social groups, in identifiable social locations, at particular moments in time. And while all human societies employ identity categories to organize interaction and structure inequality, the name, boundaries, and meaning of any one identity is a human invention and, thus, highly variable. Some identities, such as those that define race, have been constructed for the purpose of defending and justifying acts of exploitation. Others, such as those that define gender, are so deeply embedded in our institutions and cultural traditions, that they feel natural and inevitable. And still others, such as those associated

Table 2.1. Identity Meanings and Forms of Inequality at Three Levels of Analysis

| Level of Analysis | Identity Meanings | | Forms of Inequality |
	Value	Power	
Culture	Respect and prestige associated with a generalized identity category	Authority and control associated with a generalized identity category	Patterns of unequal resource distribution defined by cultural status hierarchies
Interaction	Situated deference	Situated dominance	Asymmetrical patterns of engagement evident in face-to-face encounters
Person	Self-esteem	Self-efficacy	Poor physical and psychological health; limits on autonomy and freedom

with social class, often go unnoticed even though they are central to the production of inequality.

There are many different meanings and interpretations of an identity category, but the two dimensions that have the greatest sociological significance are those associated with value and power. Some identities have more value and more power than others, and this fact has implications at the level of culture, the level of interaction, and the level of the individual person. Table 2.1 provides a visual summary of the manner in which identity meanings express inequality at these three levels of analysis.

Here it is important to recognize that culture, interaction, and person are not independent categories. I am emphasizing this formal distinction for analytical purposes only. In reality, identity meanings at the level of culture are created and maintained by actual persons engaged in face-to-face interaction. Personal identities are constructed from shared cultural meanings, and our daily interactions are structured by individual actions that are framed by meanings at the level of culture. Forms of inequality persist, in large part, because social processes at each level overlap and work together to sustain a system of power and privilege. In the following chapter, I will explore these processes in more detail and explain how identity contributes to the reproduction of inequality.

3

HOW DOES IDENTITY CONTRIBUTE TO THE REPRODUCTION OF INEQUALITY?

More than a half century ago, the people of the United States were embroiled in a contentious public debate over civil liberties and citizen rights. This was a time when segregation and discrimination on the basis of race and gender identity were common and legal. African Americans were excluded from public accommodations, blocked from equal participation in the political process, and disqualified from employment opportunities because of their "negro" identity. During this same period, most women in America also faced substantial bias and discrimination based on their gender identity: Access to advanced education and professional careers was extremely restricted, women were paid substantially less than men when working the same job, and nearly every elected political leader was male.

Most observers agree that the civil rights movements for racial justice and gender fairness were instrumental in removing significant legal barriers to equality. Petitions, mass protests, acts of civil disobedience, and years of grassroots organizing pressured a mostly white, male Congress into passing momentous federal legislation during the 1960s. The Equal Pay Act of 1963 prohibited wage differentials based on gender; the Civil Rights Act of 1964 outlawed discrimination based on race and gender in the workplace, in schools, and in other public accommodations. The Voting Rights Act of 1965 extended voting rights and banned tactics used to exclude racial minorities from the polls. And the Civil

Rights Act of 1968 advanced fair housing policies and prohibited discrimination in the sale, rental, and financing of homes.

Today we can find many indicators of greater equality for both wom-
en and blacks *because* women and African Americans now have more
access to positions and resources of power. Over the past five decades,
there has been a substantial increase in political representation by
women (20 percent of Congress in 2015), women now outnumber men
on college campuses, and nearly half of the US workforce is presently
female. Similarly, African Americans now go to the polls at a rate equivalent to that of whites, the percentage of blacks with a college degree
has more than tripled since 1960, and, of course, an African American
was elected president for the first time in 2008.

However, despite the obvious signs of progress, there are also indicators that our advance toward race and gender equality has stalled. In
1965, women were paid only 60 percent of what men were paid under
the same job classifications, and while this gap has closed over the last
fifty years, women still take home almost 20 percent less than men
when doing the same or similar work. And in some occupations, the
gender gap in pay still hovers around 60 percent: personal financial
advisers are at 61 percent, insurance agents are at 62 percent, and retail
sales associates earn only 64 percent of what their male counterparts
earn for doing the same job.[1]

For African Americans, the evidence of intransigent income inequality is even more dramatic. According to the US Census Bureau, the
median family income for black families in 1967 was only 59 percent of
the median income for white families, which means the average black
family earned 41 percent less than the average white family. In 2013,
census data showed that the income gap between black and white families had barely changed since the passing of the historic civil rights
legislation. The African American family still makes about 62 percent of
what the average white family makes in a year. And this gap is even
more severe when we examine family wealth accumulation. Between
1983 and 2013 the gap between white and black household wealth
actually *increased*. In 1983 the median net worth of white families was
ten times greater than that of black families, and by 2013 the net worth
of white households was thirteen times greater than that of the average
African American family.[2] Other indicators of a steady or growing gulf
of inequality between blacks and whites abound. The unemployment

rate for black workers continues to be twice as high as that of whites, over one-third of black children live in poverty (compared to 12 percent for whites), and the incarceration rate for black men in 2015 was three times higher than it was in 1960.[3]

Why does inequality based on race and gender identity continue to persist, and why are these identity categories still linked to social class? There is no simple answer to this question. Economic inequality is ultimately anchored in social relations of exploitation, where one social group benefits by dominating a less powerful group (the American institution of slavery is an obvious historical example), and economic exploitation based on both race and gender have been entrenched in our institutions for centuries. While the civil rights legislation of the 1960s may have outlawed some forms of discrimination and segregation, it did not dismantle the rules of capitalism, replace cultural understandings of race and gender, or erase informal practices of prejudice and discrimination. The social processes that sustain structures of inequality operate in conjunction at several different levels of analysis, and a comprehensive accounting would necessarily include a description of many different social mechanisms. In this chapter, however, I narrow our focus to the way in which identity processes contribute to the reproduction of inequality.[4]

When the American public is asked to explain the persistence of poverty and inequality, most people will reference educational deficits or character limitations.[5] Very often, these same individual faults are then associated with the characteristics of different groups. If one believes, for example, that inequality persists because poor people are unmotivated, morally weak, or ignorant, then it seems logical to conclude that African Americans and women are more likely to be poor because they can't succeed in school, don't have the same drive to achieve, or are inherently weak. This is the slippery slope of racist and sexist thinking that can occur when the social forces that sustain inequality are either hidden from view or are ignored.

The connection between identity and inequality is complex, and the persistence of this relationship over long periods of time involves multiple social forces operating at several different levels of analysis. In the following section I will take a closer look at some of these forces and show how identity-related processes help reproduce inequality at the level of culture, the level of interaction, and the level of person.

REPRODUCING INEQUALITY AT THE LEVEL OF CULTURE

Economic inequality in modern society is fundamentally tied to the forces of capitalism. Karl Marx was the first to articulate this argument more than 150 years ago, and many economists and sociologists have since provided evidence in support of this basic principle; Thomas Piketty's book (*Capital in the Twenty-First Century*) is the most famous recent contribution. There is little doubt that the rules of modern capitalism are rigged in favor of those who already have the most economic assets, receive the highest incomes, and control the most powerful institutions. Indeed, as I write these words, the richest 1 percent own and control more wealth than the bottom 50 percent of the world's population. Even Bill Gates, who has accumulated the largest fortune of any single person in the history of the world, has publicly acknowledged that "capitalism does not self-correct toward greater equality—that is, excess wealth concentration can have a snowball effect if left unchecked" and that "high levels of inequality are a problem—messing up economic incentives, tilting democracies in favor of powerful interests, and undercutting the ideal that all people are created equal."[6] We should not forget, therefore, that the reproduction of modern inequality is fundamentally tied to the operation of capitalism.

Still, inequality is not exclusively economic, and the reproduction of our particular class structure is a process that also involves shared cultural meanings attached to different identity categories—most prominently race and gender. There are certainly differences in wealth and income among women and within different racial and ethnic groups, and we know that both women and African Americans can be found among the top 1 percent of wealth owners, but the forces of domination and exploitation are not indiscriminate when it comes to race, ethnicity, and gender. Social forces clearly work to sustain a systematic process of resource distribution that is more likely to disadvantage women and persons of color. Recognizing this fact does not dismiss the very real patterns of exploitation experienced by white men, but social class is not the only basis of power and privilege; race and gender also matter. One way to get a glimpse of how identity meanings interact with economic forces is to look closely at how the labor market operates with respect to devalued identities.

This is what sociologists Joleen Kirschenman and Kathryn Neckerman were able to do in their investigation of how employers make decisions on whom to hire.[7] Specifically, they wanted to understand how identity categories associated with race, ethnicity, and class are used to inform employer evaluations and judgments of job applicants. Their study was conducted in the late 1980s and focused on businesses in Chicago and the surrounding metro area. The researchers started out by selecting a representative sample of 185 firms, and then they conducted interviews with each company's highest-ranking manager. Because race can be a sensitive topic and racial discrimination in hiring is illegal, one would expect the responses from the managers to be somewhat cautious and reserved; for this reason, the study results are likely a conservative estimate of bias.

Nevertheless, the researchers found that race was still an important factor in the hiring decisions of Chicago-area employers. When asked if it was possible to compare the work ethics of whites, blacks, and Hispanics, 38 percent of the employers said yes and ranked blacks at the bottom, while 1 percent ranked Hispanics last and none of the employers put whites last. In fact, most of those who were interviewed were willing to acknowledge that they perceive black men to be unstable, uncooperative, dishonest, and uneducated. As one respondent put it, black men have an image problem: "It's unfortunate, but in my business I think overall [black men] tend to be known as dishonest. I think that's too bad but that's the image they have . . . an image problem of being dishonest men and lazy. They're known to be lazy. They are [laughs]."[8] Here we see an example of how a devalued identity, with stereotyped meanings that are widely shared by those with power, can have real economic consequences.

Although racial identity was the primary basis for discrimination in hiring, Kirschenman and Neckerman also found that race was frequently confounded with an applicant's social class and neighborhood residence, and both class and neighborhood were taken as indicators of family background and personal values. In other words, a white identity equaled middle class, stability, and the suburbs, while black and Hispanic identities signaled inner city, unpredictability, and lower class. Consider, for example, the following quote from the owner of a construction firm: "The minority worker is not as punctual and not as concerned about punctuality as the middle-class white. So they're not as wired to the clock in keeping time and being on time as someone else who was raised in a family where the father went to work every day and the mother was up at the same time every day to make breakfast or go to work herself. It's just a cultural difference."[9]

Other employers made similar statements associating race and class with speech patterns, presentation style, and personality: "Almost all your black welfare people talk street talk" and "I find that the less skilled, the less educational background of—and now I'll say black— the more belligerent they are." Another respondent provided an example of black "culture" as threatening: "There's a certain repartee that goes on between black guys; even in this building you see it. We have a security guard and a couple of his friends that come in, I'm real uncomfortable with that. You know, I do my best to realize it's a cultural thing, but I don't like it, I don't think it's being professional, and I don't think it's the right atmosphere for the building."[10]

Class differences in speech patterns, mannerisms, and clothing style are examples of what sociologist Pierre Bourdieu has identified as *cultural capital*.[11] Many economists have argued that race and class discrimination in the labor market are due to individual differences in job skills and levels of education (*human capital*), and the traditional assumption is that identity-based discrimination will eventually disappear because competitive pressures expose the economic irrationality of such an "unproductive" bias. In other words, many economists believe discrimination is unsustainable because it is bad for business. Bourdieu, on the other hand, argues that cultural capital will often trump human capital because distinctions associated with "lifestyle" and "taste" are deeply entrenched in social relations that allow powerful individuals and groups to maintain their position of privilege and dominance.

On the face of it, there is nothing inherently "better" or "worse" when it comes to a given cultural style. Fashion, aesthetic tastes, speech patterns, accents, and vocabulary vary from person to person and group to group, and they change over time. We learn how to speak from our family, we adopt the mannerisms of those who are close to us, and we take on the habits and stylistic preferences that abound in our community. Clearly, a hip-hop rap does not sound the same as an operatic aria, French haute cuisine does not taste the same as Mexican food, and the accent of someone raised in Boston is noticeably different from the southern drawl of a lifelong resident of rural Mississippi. But difference alone is not sufficient to produce inequality. It is only after the habits and styles of one group are able to achieve dominance that cultural capital contributes to the reproduction of economic inequality. When the cultural capital of the most powerful groups is asserted as more valuable, it becomes the taken-for-granted standard against which other groups are judged. In this way, groups with different "competencies" are perceived as being deficient and lacking in the prerequisites for success.

If the cultural capital of a person with a minority group identity is unfamiliar to a business owner, if a job applicant's interaction style makes a manager uncomfortable, or if an employer deems a candidate's manner or tastes to be "not a good match," these job seekers will be at a structural disadvantage when competing in a labor market. Indeed, there is a good deal of empirical evidence to suggest that racial identity often serves as a marker of cultural capital, so that even when all pertinent qualifications are equal, racial identity is used as a differentiating factor. For example, in one study that was published in 2004, economists Marian Bertrand and Sendhil Mullainathan mailed out 1,300 paired resumes to employers in Chicago and Boston in direct response to advertised job openings.[12] These "fake" applications were identical in terms of general experience, skills, and education. However, the names on the resumes were varied so that half were stereotypical "white names" (e.g., Emily Walsh and Greg Baker), and half were stereotypical "black names" (e.g., Jamal Jones and Lakisha Washington). The results show how one's name can signal cultural capital and facilitate racial discrimination in the job market. The white-sounding names were 50 percent more likely to receive callbacks for interviews. In addition, this gap widened with resume quality; in other words, discrimination was even more severe when more highly qualified blacks were competing with more highly qualified whites.

Similar results have also been found more recently in experiments where people are trained to play the role of job applicants in real face-to-face job interviews. One study conducted in both New York City and Milwaukee, Wisconsin, for instance, had a team of equally qualified applicants with nearly identical resumes visit over three hundred employers for jobs requiring no previous experience and no education beyond high school. The results showed that white applicants were more than twice as likely as black applicants to receive callbacks or job offers in both cities (34 vs. 14 percent in Milwaukee and 31 vs. 15 percent in New York).[13] It should also be noted that in this study, the job applicants were carefully trained to offer the same style of presentation—that is, they were matched in terms of cultural capital.

If job experience, technical skills, and education (i.e., human capital) are the same for both black and white applicants, and job seekers possess the same presentation style (i.e., cultural capital), we can be confident that racial identity alone is being used to exclude access to employment. In other words, individuals in powerful social positions are using stereotyped beliefs and negative cultural meanings to reproduce economic inequality. When African Americans are devalued as "poor workers" or as "unemployable," they are excluded from jobs and segregated in the labor market; the resulting poverty and class segregation that this produces is then used as "evidence" in support of the negative cultural stereotypes and subsequent discrimination. In this way, devalued racial identities become a self-fulfilling prophecy.

A similar process of identity discrimination, exclusion, and segregation in the labor market also contributes to the reproduction of gender inequality.[14] We see this, for example, in a small study of restaurant hiring practices in Philadelphia.[15] Researchers had four equally trained and matched college students (two men and two women) apply for jobs as waitstaff at sixty-five different restaurants. Each restaurant received an application from one man and one woman, for a total of 130 applications. Overall, the male applicants were on average 40 percent more likely to receive both a callback interview and a job offer. What makes this study even more interesting is that gender discrimination was significantly more likely to occur in the high-priced restaurants, where wages and tips are much greater. This shows how bias against women within a particular employment sector can also contribute to income inequality.

Another interesting test of gender-based employment discrimination was conducted by economists Claudia Goldin and Cecilia Rouse.[16] These researchers examined the hiring procedures of the major US orchestras over a fifty-year period. Prior to the 1970s, auditions occurred in full view of the hiring committee, but by the late 1980s most every orchestra had adopted a procedure wherein auditions took place behind a screen so that the musician's identity was unknown to the evaluating jury. Goldin and Rouse wanted to know if this change in practice was effective in reducing a perceived bias against women performers.

Orchestras have a long history of being dominated by men, and some people have argued that this difference is more a reflection of talent than it is an indicator of bias; meaning that women are less likely to be hired simply because they are less skilled. But when Goldin and Rouse analyzed orchestra records they found that the proportion of women being hired jumped substantially with the implementation of blind auditions. In fact, their statistical analysis estimates that the probability of a woman being hired increased by 50 percent with the adoption of screens.

Prior to the civil rights legislation of the 1960s it was common for employers to specify gender and race preferences in their job notices. The following advertisements, published in 1960, are typical of notices that appeared during this era:[17]

> WAITRESS—White. Good tips. 7611-15 Stoney Island RE 4-
> 8837. (*Chicago Tribune*, 1960)
> DRIVERS (TRUCK). Colored, for trash routes; over 25 years of
> age; paid vacation, year-around work; must have excellent
> driving record. Apply SHAYN BROS. 1601 W St. NE. (*Washington Post*, 1960)
> HOUSEKEEPER—European or Oriental—2 adults, pri. quarters, under 45. Ref. GR, 2-4891. (*Los Angeles Times*, 1960)
> COUPLE, $400-500, white for business couple with 2 adult children. Private home Forest Hills. Man to work in business. BO
> 3-2649. (*New York Times*, 1960)

Employer preferences reflected stereotypical meanings and prejudicial beliefs that were dominant at the time, and because the vast majority of employers were white and male, these identity barriers worked to reproduce gender and racial inequalities. Banning the use of identity preferences in job announcements has reduced some forms of employment discrimination and has no doubt softened the expression of the more egregious gender and racial stereotypes, but negative cultural meanings are only the tip of the inequality iceberg. Beneath the surface lies a much larger and more complex structure of interaction where meanings are sustained, beliefs are reproduced, and discrimination is normalized.

REPRODUCING INEQUALITY AT THE LEVEL
OF INTERACTION

A curious feature of the job listings and hiring patterns prior to 1964 is that many announcements actually specified a preference *for* women and racial minorities. We see this, for example, in the listings above that advertise for "colored" trash collectors and "white waitresses." In these instances, we find evidence of discrimination that had at times served to limit the labor market opportunities of white men so as to preserve an idealized view of "women's work" and "negro labor." Of course, the jobs that were reserved for individuals with devalued identities involved labor that was also devalued, meaning that high-status occupations excluded women and racial and ethnic minorities, while many low-status occupations excluded poor white men.

Even though race and gender discrimination in hiring has been against the law for more than a half century, many historical patterns of occupational segregation persist to this day. Sophisticated statistical analyses of job type, gender, race, and ethnic identity shows, for example, that women are more likely than men to be segregated into certain occupations, and nonwhites are more likely to be segregated than whites. Moreover, these differences hold even when individual levels of human capital (i.e., job skills, education, language proficiency) are taken into account. This means that even when individual job qualifications are held constant, African Americans and Native Americans are much more likely than other racial-ethnic groups to be concentrated in lower-paying occupations. Moreover, when gender is added to the equation, we find that Hispanic women become the most likely to be segregated into low-paying jobs.[18]

If education and job skills can't account for these differences, what can? The answer to this question is not simple. We know that there are numerous macroeconomic forces in the global economy that contribute to migration flows and the persistence of segregationist labor patterns, and we know that these forces can work differently for different occupation groups.[19] But one critical factor that is often overlooked has to do with the power of identity and the reproduction of inequality at the level of interaction. The segregation of women and ethnic minorities into low-paying jobs persists in part because it serves the economic interests of employers and elevates the value and power of white, native-born Americans. We can illustrate how identity works in this regard if we focus on the case of *domestic labor*, where housekeepers, nannies, and caregivers continue to be disproportionally female, nonwhite, and foreign born.[20]

Domestic Labor and Inequality at the Level of Interaction

The segregation of poor, nonwhite, and immigrant women into domestic labor has a long history in the United States. During the latter part of the nineteenth century, most domestics who were hired to work in the growing industrial cities of the North and Midwest were young female immigrants from Ireland. Working as a house servant or live-in domestic was at the time considered one of the most demeaning and undignified occupations available to a young woman.[21] Cleaning, sewing, and caring for another family's children was so odious and stigmatizing that native born white women in need of work refused to labor in homes, preferring instead the lower wages and unsafe conditions of the mills and factories. The high demand for domestics in the United States was one factor the attracted immigrants from Ireland, and by the end of the nineteenth century, so many servants were Irish that the demeaning nature of the work was often associated with the perceived shortcomings of the Irish "race," a point well illustrated in the following representative quote retrieved from a historical document comparing Irish and Italian immigrant workers:

> The Irish are about the only race which can be said to prefer housework. In general they desire positions of this sort, but the influx of Irish immigrants is past and now it is a very small stream which comes when compared to the hordes which came before the Italian invasion. Italians do not take kindly to housework.[22]

The segregation of Irish women into domestic labor eventually dissipated in the early part of the twentieth century, when nativist immigration policies restricted the flow of women from Ireland. To meet the demand for domestics, African American women from the South were recruited to take the place of the Irish immigrants, and by the middle of the twentieth century over 80 percent of black women in the labor force were employed in domestic service. The dominance of native-born African American women in cleaning, cooking, and childcare was in large part a legacy of slavery, and this particular pattern of segregated labor continued up into the 1960s before employment opportunities for African American women opened up and new streams of poor immigrants were recruited to take their place in domestic labor. Today, the demand for domestics is as strong as it has ever been, and the demographic distribution of domestic workers generally reflects regional differences in immigration flows. In the Northeast, for example, Caribbean-born women are a predominant part of the labor pool of domestics; in the West, Latino and Asian women are overrepresented; and in the cities and towns of the Midwest, we find a mix of different racial and ethnic groups. One constant over the last century, however, has been that the vast majority of housekeepers, maids, and home care providers continue to be nonwhite, female, and poor.[23]

Segregation in terms of gender, ethnicity, and race in domestic service jobs is an example of how inequality in the labor market is tied to particular identities. Domestic labor has historically been low-paying, demanding in time and energy, and exempt from many of the legal regulations afforded other occupations. To be employed as a domestic has meant accepting work that is widely considered demeaning and undignified. It has meant working under conditions isolated from other workers and often in the presence of a family of superiors and supervisors. For these reasons, it is an undesirable occupation and remains one of the few jobs available to young women who immigrate to the United States. But if we are to fully understand how this form of inequality is reproduced and reinforced, we need to examine the manner in which identity works to frame the dynamics of interpersonal behavior within the household.

When the Irish and Caribbean immigrants sailed to the United States, when former slaves migrated north and west from their plantations, when Latinos crossed the northern border of Mexico, and when Filipinos and other Asians traversed the Pacific, they carried with them distinct accents, lifestyles, and skin colors that marked their class position and signaled their "difference" from the families whom they were hired to serve. In this way, the physical and cultural symbols of identity operate as "status signs" that are often used like a worker's uniform to clarify boundaries between family and nonfamily in intimate surroundings, where distinguishing between employer and employee is not always obvious.

According to historian David Katzman, employers initially showed a preference for women of color because of their "invisibility":

> One peculiar and most degrading aspect of domestic service was the requisite of invisibility. The ideal servant . . . would be invisible and silent, responsive to demands but deaf to gossip, household chatter and conflicts, attentive to needs of mistress and master but blind to their faults, sensitive to the moods and whims of those around them but undemanding of family warmth, love and security. Only blacks could be invisible people in white homes.[24]

In addition, because the gender and racial identities of most domestics are already culturally devalued, dominance and control by a white employer are easier to manage, less interpersonally challenging, and feels more "natural." As a result, everyday interactions between a domestic worker and her employer are often stained with indignities. We see this, for example, in the experience of Maribel Centeno, a twenty-two-year-old immigrant from Guatemala City, who worked as a live-in nanny and housekeeper. In an interview with sociologist Pierrette Hondagneu-Sotelo, she summarized her experience by saying: "The pay was bad. The treatment was, how shall I say? It was cordial, a little, uh, not racist, but with very little consideration, very little respect."[25]

Ms. Centeno's experience is not uncommon, and other studies have documented similar degrading relationships. When sociologist Mary Romero interviewed domestics in the Denver, Colorado, area, a Chicana housecleaner had this to say about her employers:

> Some of them were really hateful. They thought you know, you're just anybody there to clean their house and they really would take advantage of you. And I didn't enjoy it. . . . I don't know if it was just cause they thought you know, that you were Spanish and stuff, they would just sort of take advantage of me and I didn't like it.[26]

Given the interpersonally demeaning nature of domestic work, it is not surprising that a Los Angeles area domestic workers' coalition lists as their number-one priority "Respect for our rights and dignity as a person. We don't want to be ignored and humiliated."[27]

All persons possess an inherent dignity, but as the examples above show, social relationships are not necessarily structured in a manner that recognizes or enhances our common humanity. Indifference and disrespect are not natural predispositions, and status, prestige, and power do not emerge organically from one's self. To sustain a system of inequality requires work. Identities must be socially constructed, and the meanings associated with an identity must be continuously reinforced. When a domestic worker is disrespected or ignored, her humanity has been diminished and her inherent dignity has been denied, but such acts of humiliation also serve to simultaneously reinforce the relative power and value of identity categories. In sociological terms, acts of degradation instantiate a microstructure of inequality.

According to sociologist Erving Goffman, face-to-face behavior is organized around a series of interpersonal rituals that form a system of deference "in which an actor celebrates and confirms his [*sic*] relation to a recipient" as "seen most clearly in the little salutations, compliments and apologies which punctuate social intercourse."[28] While these seemingly mundane acts of common courtesy may appear to be trivial or inconsequential, Goffman argues that they serve as the microfoundation for social order. Although each individual may deserve deference by virtue of being a person, one is not allowed to give it to oneself and must instead seek respect and admiration from others. This is a critical observation. Goffman reasons that "if the individual could give himself the deference he desired there might be a tendency for society to disintegrate into islands inhabited by solitary cultish men, each in continuous worship at his own shrine."[29]

Contrary to the message of a widely used aphorism that proclaims, "No one can make you feel inferior without your consent,"[30] feelings of power and powerlessness do in fact emerge from social relationships and are dependent upon the actions, evaluations, and comments of others. Even small gestures, such as a timely smile, an acknowledgment of work well done, an inquiry about another's health, or a simple thank-you, are sizeable in their impact. They are significant because they are rituals that affirm the dignity of the person, and when strung together these ceremonies of interaction serve to verify the legitimacy of one's identity.

But before one can receive deference from another, one must first display the appropriate *demeanor*. An insubordinate maid, a defiant servant, or an unruly caretaker will not garner the positive salutations and deferential gestures one desires and expects. It is only when one presents an appropriately respectful disposition that an appropriate deference is returned. In this way, a system of deference and demeanor favors the status quo and works to reproduce the dominant social order. To act against an existing status hierarchy risks embarrassment and anxiety for all involved. If an employee fails to display a subservient or compliant demeanor, she risks being viewed as uppity, cocky, pretentious, or insolent, and an employer who is too overbearing and imperious risks being viewed as haughty, ungrateful, cold, or insensitive. But of course, presentation of an "unacceptable" demeanor by actors at the bottom of a status hierarchy is much riskier than the inappropriate demeanor of someone at the top of a status hierarchy.

Working as a domestic means living on the edge of poverty, and upsetting an employer can mean losing one's job—a crushing economic blow for most domestics. Employers, on the other hand, risk losing an employee and might face the inconvenience of a having to find a replacement, but their economic security and class position remain unchanged. While both employer and employee are making a claim for dignity and basic personhood, the differences in power and value associated with their respective identities mean that the domestic worker has more "skin in the game" and more dignity at stake. The fact that costs are higher for the domestic worker also means that she has greater pressure to conform and that she will find it much more difficult to resist an established system of deference and demeanor—even if her dignity as a person is being assaulted. Yet, when employees look to avoid confrontation, seek validation for devalued identities, and engage in a form of interaction that preserves the interaction order, they are indirectly reproducing inequality.

Persons with devalued identities may also have a more direct hand in the reproduction of inequality at the level of interaction. Sometimes, for example, members of a subordinate group will disparage others who share the very same identity in an attempt to improve their own relative status. Sociologist Michael Schwalbe and colleagues refer to this interactional strategy as *defensive othering*.[31] Ethnographic research has found evidence, for instance, of homeless men who belittle others on the street for being lazy, women criticizing other women for being too masculine, and Irish immigrants disparaging other Irish for being heavy drinkers. In each of these examples, the intentional distancing of one's own self from a devalued identity serves to legitimate the negative stereotypes associated with the less powerful identity. With defensive othering we can see the unintended consequences of negative identity meanings that are accepted and internalized at the level of the person.

REPRODUCING INEQUALITY AT THE PERSON LEVEL

Identity categories have common cultural interpretations and meanings that emerge from social relationships. When relationships become exploitative, some identities develop more value and power than others, and these symbolic inequalities are then reinforced and buttressed by systems of deference and demeanor at the level of interaction. Over time, identity meanings can be internalized by individuals, influencing the way we think, affecting how we feel, and guiding our perceptions of the social world. This is especially evident when it comes to gender, race, and age, where identity is easily attributed and inequality is often prominent.

In fact, sociologist Cecilia Ridgeway has argued that the near universal persistence of gender inequality is derived from our collective reliance on gender identity as a "primary frame" for organizing our most fundamental social activities. Unlike everyday identities associated with work, religion, or family, for example, one's gender identity is nearly ubiquitous in its salience across situations. In other words, gender is always and everywhere in the background, and it serves as a basic starting point in almost every encounter. Because of this, the cultural meanings associated with gender are difficult to contain, and "the use of gender as a framing device spreads gendered meanings, including assumptions about inequality embedded in those meanings, to all spheres of social life that are carried out through social relationships." As a consequence, "gender inequality is rewritten into new economic and social arrangements as they emerge, preserving inequality in modified form over socioeconomic transformations."[32]

The important point being made here is that gender inequality is not simply the reflection of positive or negative identity meanings. If this were the case, a change in attitude and a more enlightened view of gender differences would be sufficient to end gender inequality. Rather, gender inequality persists because gender identity is simultaneously built into institutional positions where men are more likely to have greater power and access to valued resources. From the structure of the family to the structure of the corporation, men are more likely to be in control, and when gender differences are consistently noticed and experienced at the level of everyday interaction, discriminatory identity meanings are reinforced. A male identity is assumed to have higher value and greater power largely *because* men are more likely to be found in positions of authority and in roles with greater status. In other words, traditional gender stereotypes will persist as long as people's daily experience serves to confirm widely held cultural beliefs about women as having less competence and deserving of less esteem than men.

A compelling body of empirical research supports Ridgeway's explanation for the staying power of gender inequality, and additional evidence suggests a somewhat similar process at work when it comes to identities defined by race and age. For example, cognitive psychologists who investigate the way we process perceptual images have found that categories associated with race, gender, and age are unique in that they function as "primary categories" in the recognition of others.[33] Primary categories are fundamental cognitive schemas that facilitate the processing of information and operate so quickly that they require little (if any) conscious thought. This means that the perception of race, gender, and age is often an involuntary response that precedes the recognition of other identities.

Before a job applicant is ever interviewed, before a political candidate ever gives a speech, or before a suspect is ever questioned by police, each one is first recognized as either a "young black man," a "middle-aged Latina," or an "elderly white male." This automatic processing of information then becomes the lens through which more detailed and conscious perceptions are organized and interpreted.

Of course, if the unconscious recognition of race, gender, and age was simply a matter of difference and was associated with extraneous or neutral cultural meanings, this basic cognitive processing of information would be largely irrelevant to inequality. But in fact, evidence shows that primary categories are not immune to the cultural interpretations of value and power. When someone is automatically categorized, the cultural meanings associated with the category are simultaneously invoked, and these very first interpretations then set the stage for all subsequent interactions. In this way, gender and racial stereotypes "get a head start" in the framing of everyday interactions. Even when we are committed to consciously rejecting negative representations, automatic stereotyping at a subconscious level may still influence our perception and evaluation of others.

A large number of experiments have demonstrated the subtle way in which prejudice and bias continue to operate even among individuals who formally express egalitarian attitudes.[34] For example, in one study, white students at a university were asked to evaluate job candidates who had applied for a position as a peer counselor at the university. Unbeknown to the students, the race and qualifications of the candidates were systematically manipulated by the researchers. One-third of the candidates had credentials that were very strong, one-third had moderate credentials, and one-third possessed very weak qualifications. The results showed no evidence of racial discrimination on the part of the white students when the job candidates had either very strong qualifications or very weak qualifications. However, when the candidate's credentials were more ambiguous, (the moderate condition), the white students were much more likely to recommend the white candidate over the black candidate (76 percent vs. 45 percent) even though the credentials were essentially identical. In other words, when the correct decision was less obvious, white students appeared to give the white candidate the benefit of the doubt.

What makes this experiment especially notable is that it was conducted twice on the same university campus—once during the 1988–1989 academic year and again during the 1998–1999 academic year. In both instances, the study participants completed a questionnaire that assessed their racial attitudes before participating in the experiment. While the results showed a significant decline in expressed racial bias over the ten-year period, there was, in fact, no difference in the white students' preference for the white job candidates. This means that the subtle and unconscious form of identity bias was more persistent.[35]

Some argue that these deep cognitive structures are evolutionary in their origin, while others believe that they are learned sometime during the first two years of a child's development, but whatever their source, the existence of primary categories helps explain why certain identity inequalities are more likely to persist. Still, we must keep in mind that inequality is not an inevitable outcome of identity categorization. If inequality is to be sustained, the shared cultural meaning of an identity must also be devalued, degraded, and disempowered, and these de-graded meanings must also be legitimated in our institutions and rein-forced in our face-to-face encounters. There is nothing inevitable or natural in the fact that low-paying, low-status jobs are segregated by gender and race. And even when these identities are rooted in deep cognitive categories, the meanings associated with any particular iden-tity are never permanent; rather, they remain open to change.

Another reason for the intransigence of certain inequalities is that identity meanings and cultural stereotypes establish a set of generalized expectations for the types of feelings and actions we can expect to experience in any given encounter. Knowing someone's identity helps frame a situation and allows for a certain degree of predictability as well as a measure of comfort in knowing what to expect—even when the likely outcome is not necessarily just or fair. In fact, sociologists have found that much of our interpersonal behavior is guided by emotions, sentiments, and feelings that come to be associated with certain iden-tities in certain social contexts. When there is a discrepancy between what we expect to feel and what we actually experience in a given situation, we will be motivated to reduce the incongruity by trying to make our actions and feelings consistent with the cultural meanings and expectations associated with the social setting. *Affect control theory*, originally developed by sociologist David R. Heise, describes how this interpersonal control system operates.[36]

Affect Control Theory and the Reproduction of Inequality

Imagine you are looking for work and receive an invitation to a prelimi-nary job interview. How should you dress? Should you wear a suit and a pair of dress shoes or should you wear something more casual? How should you act? Should you present yourself as confident, assertive, and creative, or would it be better to appear reserved, gentle, and attentive? The answer to these questions will likely depend on your sense of what the employer expects, and employer expectations will be closely aligned with the type of job for which you are being considered. A job interview at a law firm for a position as an attorney, for example, will call for a style of presentation quite different from, say, a job interview as a farm laborer, nurse's aide, or domestic servant. An assertive demeanor and stylish business suit might work in your favor during the job interview for the attorney position, but it could work against your chances of landing work as a farm laborer or as a domestic.

This point is well illustrated by sociologist Judith Rollins, who conducted a lengthy study of domestic workers in the Greater Boston area. Part of her research involved collecting data as a "participant observer" while working as a domestic for ten different employers. Rollins (who is African American) was especially interested in understanding how class and race informed the relationship between a female employer and a female employee. The following passage describes Professor Rollins's experience in being hired for one of her jobs:

> Although Ms. Canton and I had agreed at our interview that I would start working for her the following week, she called me the night before I was to begin and expressed hesitancy about hiring me because "you seem so well educated." Because I had completed my first set of domestic jobs, I had, in fact, gone to this interview somewhat carelessly relaxed: I carried myself and spoke in a natural way, without the deliberately subservient manner I had feigned during my first set of job interviews (when I questioned if I could successfully pass myself off as a domestic). Because her call caused me concern about retaining the job, I arrived the following day looking especially shabby (baggy slacks, old work shirt, cotton headscarf tied Southern-style) and with an exaggeratedly subservient demeanor (standing less erect, eyes usually averted from hers, a tentativeness of movement). Most important, I said almost nothing, asked the few necessary questions in a soft unassertive voice, and responded to her directions with "Yes, Ma'am." I was rather shocked at her obvious pleasure over and total lack of suspicion about this performance, especially since she had encountered me without it the previous week. To me I felt like an absurd and transparent caricature of Stepin Fetchit; her mind, however, was clearly eased of the apprehensions she had had about my suitability for the job. She did not question the change; my behavior now expressed my belief in my inferiority in relation to her and thus my acceptance of her superiority in relation to me. Her desire for that confirmation from me was apparently strong enough to erase from her memory the contradiction of my previous behavior.[37]

Rollins's position as a sociologist seeking employment as a domestic worker may be unusual, but her decision to conform to the identity stereotype of her employer is a predictable response that has been more generally described and mathematically modeled under affect control theory.

The basic principles of affect control theory are rather straightforward and are consistent with the central features of identity meaning described in chapter 2. The theory begins with the assumption that every social event demands a "definition of the situation" that includes an understanding of (1) the actor identities, (2) the ongoing behavior, (3) the object of the behavior, and (4) the nature of the setting. The theory also assumes that every situation generates a basic set of emotions or affective response. If a specific combination of identities, behavior, objects, and settings is consistent with cultural expectations, then positive feelings emerge. But if one's impression of a particular event is inconsistent or discrepant on any one element or combination of elements, actors are motivated to reduce the discrepancy. For example, an "event" might involve a teacher (actor identity) praising (behavior) a student (actor identity) in a classroom (setting). In this case, the definition of the situation appears consistent with widely shared cultural expectations, and, as a result, positive sentiments are generated. However, if we change the behavior so that the teacher is now kissing the student in the classroom, our impression is dramatically altered, we experience an uncomfortable affective response, and we will most likely search for a way to restore consistency.

Sometimes we restore positive emotions by redefining the situation with an alternative interpretation. Perhaps our initial impression was wrong. We might, for example, discover that the "teacher" is in fact the father of the student or that the "kiss" was really a whisper in the ear of the student. But if *redefinition* is not possible, we will need to take corrective action to restore positive sentiments. We might, for example, intervene and confront the teacher about the incident, report our observation to authorities, or contact the child's family. Either way, through corrective actions or reinterpretation, the discrepancy is resolved, positive sentiments are restored, and cultural expectations are affirmed.

When Ms. Canton first interviewed Professor Rollins, she had a negative emotional experience. Something about the initial job interview didn't seem right to Ms. Canton because domestic workers should not "seem so well educated." But after Professor Rollins changed her clothes and altered her demeanor, consistency among identity, action, and setting were reestablished, Ms. Canton became satisfied, and Professor Rollins was hired. In this way, the system of affect control operates in a manner similar to the temperature setting on a thermostat, where sentiments at the cultural level serve as a general reference or standard for particular situational experiences. When the social situation gives rise to discrepant feelings and impressions, a control process is activated so as to maintain stability in the system.

Sociologists using affect control theory employ a rigorous methodology to measure cultural meanings of identities and the sentiments they produce in particular situations. This information is then used to formulate mathematical models and computer simulations of human behavior in a range of settings and for an array of identities. As a result, researchers have amassed hundreds of quantitative studies that confirm the basic principles of the theory.[38] Most critically, this body of research shows that human social behavior has a tendency to maintain and reproduce prevailing cultural expectations about identity and social behavior.

Individuals engaged in ordinary everyday interaction have a tendency to seek identity confirmation and avoid identity disruptions. As a result, established systems of inequality are often reproduced even though they work to disadvantage most people.

Affect control theory is primarily concerned with the maintenance of a common *definition of the situation* where actor identities are one part of a larger, more complex, equation. However, other theorists have used similar cybernetic control models to show how we are also motivated to achieve stability and personal self-consistency at the individual level. For example, sociologist Peter Burke and his colleagues have shown that we also use *identity standards* as a guide when steering our own behavior in social settings. In other words, the internal dynamics of a single identity has its own cybernetic control system. If feedback from others is consistent with the identity standard, we feel good about our self, but if others' response is incongruent with the stable meanings associated with an identity (the standard), negative emotions such as depression or anger will be aroused. When an identity cannot be verified during a social encounter, corrective action will usually be taken in an attempt to confirm one's sense of self and restore stability to the system.

Here it is important to emphasize that inequality influences the operation of the feedback loop. Identities with less value and power will be subject to greater control from others and will have a limited capacity for independence and agency. We see this, for example, in a study that found that, among newly married couples, spouses with less powerful identities outside of marriage (less education, lower-prestige occupations) were more likely to have their self-meanings influenced by a higher-status spouse. On the other hand, spouses with higher-status identities reported self-meanings that were relatively independent of their lower-status partner.[39] Thus, not only does the identity control process lean toward stability and the reproduction of existing structural arrangements, but it also reinforces the power and privilege associated with more highly valued identities.

SUMMARY

Economic inequality occurs when one social group benefits from the domination of a less powerful group. Once economic exploitation is established, it is often reinforced and legitimated through the construction of identity categories. We see this most clearly in the use of race and gender, two identity categories that have been associated with prejudice and discrimination in numerous societies for many centuries. In this chapter I have argued that the persistence of inequality is due in large part to identity-related processes at three distinct levels of analysis. At the level of culture, inequality is sustained when the value and power of an identity category is assumed to be natural, legitimate, or just. When inequality is either invisible, passed off as acceptable, or dismissed as inconsequential, there is no pressure to alter the meaning of devalued identity categories, and the momentum of habit and tradition carries inequality forward. At the level of interaction, I have argued that interpersonal systems of deference and demeanor reinforce the status quo and bolster exploitative relationships. When we work to avoid confrontation, seek validation for a devalued identity, and participate in an interaction exchange that preserves an expected interaction order, we are indirectly reproducing structures of inequality. And finally, at the level of the person, I have argued that cognitive processes and emotional control systems motivate individual actions and combine to strengthen established identity meanings. Most of us want to avoid experiencing negative sentiments, and most of us desire stable and predictable identities, but these personal preferences often have the unintended consequence of sustaining one's position in relationships of inequality—even in circumstances where we recognize that we are being exploited.

Altering dominant cultural meanings of devalued identities is not impossible, but changing the cultural standard (the setting on the thermostat), disrupting interpersonal systems of deference and demeanor, and creating new identity relations typically require collective action over a long period of time. For this to occur, identities that are being used to demean and disparage must somehow be converted into sources of pride, dignity, and solidarity. Indeed, clearing a path toward liberation and positive social change is possible *because* identities are not simply cogs in an inequality machine; identities can also serve as resources for resistance and reform. In the following chapter I will take a closer look at the process of emancipation and explore the manner in which identity can also work to disrupt and transform established systems of power and privilege.

4

HOW IS IDENTITY USED TO
RESIST INEQUALITY?

As we navigate our way through life, we seek out the safe harbors and solid moorings of recognizable identities, established meanings, and predictable interactions. These are the comfortable and familiar social shelters where a secure sense of self is most easily realized. In chapter 3 I showed how this desire for security is a factor in the reproduction of inequality. As humans, we have a highly developed capacity for self-consciousness and self-reflection —a skill that sets us apart from other species and enables enormous amounts of creativity and invention. But this ability to see ourselves as objects, evaluate our actions, and assess our place in the world also comes with a troubling amount of existential anxiety. Because we have the capacity for self-reflection, we think about and question our own existence, we worry about what others think of us, and we wonder what the future holds in life and in death. As a consequence, we have a fundamental motivation to experience the routine, the regular, and the normative, and as we strive for security, we unintentionally reproduce the status quo.

But does our desire for predictability mean that structures of inequality are impervious to change? Is the concentration of power therefore a permanent and inevitable consequence of our human nature? In this chapter I will argue that the answer to both questions is a resounding *no!* The desire for predictability, structure, and stability is a compelling force indeed, but it is not our only source of motivation. We also have basic biological motives to satiate hunger and thirst, seek shelter against the elements, and avoid physical harm. In addition, a fully developed and socially mature self is also motivated to achieve dignity and avoid exploitation. But our biological, psychological, and sociological systems do not always work in harmony. When the regular and predictable social system fails to meet our physical needs, or produces exploitation and feelings of indignity, this contradiction in motives can spark resistance and positive social change.

Indeed, this is the paradox of emancipation: To achieve the stability of a more just social system, we must first disrupt the stability of an unjust system. Inequality may be pervasive and persistent, but it is neither natural nor inevitable. Power structures may offer predictability and stability, but this does not mean that we always and everywhere accept indignity. History is replete with examples of long-standing power structures that "unexpectedly" crumble under the weight of injustice. In other words, endurance should not be confused with permanence.

Resistance is never easy. Challenging long-standing structures of inequality can be uncomfortable, frightening, and dangerous, especially for individuals acting alone. Yet despite the obvious risks, we find that individual frustrations and grievances are quite often converted into collective acts of reform and revolution. Positive social change is possible because the very same human capacities for symbolic interaction and identity construction that are used to establish and legitimate structures of inequality prove to be valuable resources in the struggle to eliminate unjust differences in income, wealth, power, prestige, and privilege.

The road to emancipation is never short or straight, and there are no guide maps or signposts to provide direction. We do know, however, that the power of identity is an essential resource along the way. Other social forces are also implicated, of course, and we should not lose sight of the fact that identity processes are embedded within a much larger social system, but resistance, reform, and revolution cannot occur independent of identity processes. Wherever agitation for justice occurs, and whenever greater equality is achieved, we can be certain that identity processes are serving as a crucial resource.

In this chapter I will review the relationship between identity and resistance at the level of culture, the level of interaction, and the level of the person. These are the same three levels of analysis I used to explain the reproduction of inequality in chapter 3. I want to begin, however, with a more general discussion of research on the way in which children respond to inequality. For it is in the examination of children's reaction to injustice that we find the beginnings of our own adult motivations to advocate for human dignity.

THE REJECTION OF INEQUALITY BY CHILDREN

Our ability to understand and appreciate the difference between a fair and an unjust distribution of valued resources emerges very early in life. In fact, a mounting body of empirical research by developmental psychologists suggests that children as young as eighteen months have the ability to recognize fairness in the distribution of rewards. Additional research shows that by the age of three, children will become disturbed when they perceive that an injustice has occurred, and they will be motivated to reduce perceived inequities, even if it is at their own expense.

We see this, for example, in a study where children between the ages of three and eight were invited to play a game with an experimenter. Once the game was over, the following statement was made by the experimenter (the statement was manipulated to test for gender differences):

> Thanks for playing this game with me. We want to give you some erasers for doing such a good job answering questions. We want to give some erasers to you and to another little boy (girl) named Mark (Mary). The problem is I don't know how many erasers to give to both of you. Can you help me with that? Great. You get to decide how many erasers you and Mark (Mary) will get. We have these five erasers. We have one for you, one for Mark (Mary), one for you, and one for Mark (Mary). Uh oh! We have one left over. Then children were asked, "Should I give this eraser to you, or should I throw it away?"[1]

Surprisingly, more than 80 percent of children chose to preserve equity by throwing the extra eraser away (no gender differences were found).

In a similar experiment, pairs of children (unfamiliar to each other) were invited to play a game in which one participant was allowed to control a machine that distributed Skittles candies, while a second child sat on the other side of the machine facing the operator. Following a series of questions, the experimenter placed either an equitable or an inequitable distribution of candy on a chute attached to the machine. The decider was then asked to pull one of two levers that would either accept the allocation (both participants receive candy) or reject the allocation (neither child receives candy). Consistent with other research, it was found that children were most likely to forego the candy if the allocation disadvantaged their partner. But in this study, the researchers also found that the rejection of inequity occurred only when a partner was physically present; when the game was played without a partner, inequity was considered acceptable—a finding that highlights the important influence of social relationships.[2]

The significance of social relationships has also been demonstrated in a series of other experiments where researchers found that children were much more likely to share stickers if they believed that the recipient was either needy (feels sad or has few toys) or morally deserving (shares with other children and does not push).[3] Overall, this line of research is consistent with the argument (presented in chapter 2) that perspective-taking, empathy, and altruism are distinctive features of human development. These are capacities that coincide with language development and the emergence of the self. Without a fully developed self, our perspective on the world is narrow and egocentric, and we have little concern for justice and fairness. As we mature physically and socially, we become more sensitive to the plight of others, we begin to recognize a fair resource distribution, and we are upset if erasers, candies, and stickers are not distributed equally.

It is heartening to know that a motivation to establish equality and fairness develops at a very young age, but inequality in the adult world is obviously more complex, more diverse, and more difficult to recognize. In addition, the resources valued by adults go well beyond stickers, candy, and erasers to include more expensive consumer products, entertainment, personal services, and cash. We also desire intangible and symbolic resources such as status, prestige, respect, and recognition, which are less objective, more difficult to compare, and opaque in their origin.

Before one can reject a social arrangement as unfair, one must first believe an injustice exists—something that is never as simple as counting the number of candies on a plate. In the real world, perception of fairness is often distorted by false interpretations of who is in need, and biased assessments of moral worth. As a consequence, anger can be hard to generate, motivation can be difficult to harness, and resistance can be tough to organize. Nevertheless, there are moments of clarity in our lives when we do recognize the causes of inequality and decide to fight back. One of the best examples of this is found in the modern labor movement.

INEQUALITY AND RESISTANCE IN THE LABOR MOVEMENT

Most of us accept the fact that there are massive differences among workers in terms of salary and wages. Doctors on average make more than nurses, teachers make more than school bus drivers, store managers earn more than cashiers, and the CEO of a global agribusiness will take home more than the head of a small family farm. These income gaps don't usually bother the average person. Inequality of this type is typically justified as legitimate compensation for different degrees of skill, education, experience, or "hard work." For some of us, even the colossal paychecks given to star athletes, entertainers, and corporate CEOs are rationalized as the natural outcome of a competitive market. But there are two conditions under which most people are less accepting of wage inequality. We can refer to these conditions as *absolute deprivation* and *relative deprivation*.

Absolute deprivation occurs when a person's compensation is insufficient to live a healthy and safe life. Someone who can't pay the rent, put food on the table, or care for a sick child will likely become angry, frustrated, and motivated to demand more for his or her labor. Relative deprivation, on the other hand, occurs when a person realizes that other people who are similarly situated are being more generously compensated for the same labor. One may be earning a wage sufficient to purchase comfort and security, but if the wage is not fair or just, relative to other workers, a different type of anger and frustration will occur. The experience of both forms of deprivation has been a catalyst for the labor movement.

The labor movement in the United States can be traced to the eighteenth century, in the colonial period before the revolution. In those early days, artisans and craftworkers organized to fight for shorter work-days and against wage reductions. In this period prior to the rise of the factory system, most union activists were skilled in a particular trade such as shoemaking, carpentry, or printing. But by the early twentieth century, a new industrial economy was taking shape, and millions of new immigrants were arriving to meet the demand for unskilled labor. It was during this period that union organizing expanded to the mills, mines, and factories, where most of the new laborers toiled away for long hours under dangerous conditions and for poverty wages. This was also a period of growing class-consciousness and a deeper appreciation of the common interests shared by all exploited workers.

With greater numbers and growing solidarity, the political power of unions began to take hold, and new legal protections were gradually won for all employees—unionized or not. These improvements in-cluded restrictions on child labor, the establishment of an eight-hour workday, a forty-hour workweek, health and safety regulations in the workplace, minimum-wage laws, and protections against discrimination based on race, ethnicity, gender, and religion.

The transformative impact of the labor movement on the US econo-my is undeniable, and there is little doubt that labor unions have been a positive force in the reduction of economic inequality. In figure 4.1 the bottom trend line offers a historical snapshot of the rise and decline of union membership over the past one hundred years. The second trend line, on the top, traces the corresponding variation in income inequality (the concentration of income in the hands of the top 10 percent). When union membership was at its peak during the 1950s, economic inequal-ity (in terms of income) was at its lowest point. Since that time, union membership has declined and income inequality has increased.

It should also be noted that this effect is not limited to the US economy. When we plot rates of union membership for other countries we find a positive association with multiple indicators of inequality, suggesting that strong and influential labor unions are key to creating and sustaining social equality.[4] We also know that in the United States, at least, the decline of union membership has had the effect of reducing average wages for both black and white men and has increased the wage gap between black and white women.[5]

Why is this? Why do labor unions reduce economic inequality? The most obvious answer is that unions have the ability to negotiate wage

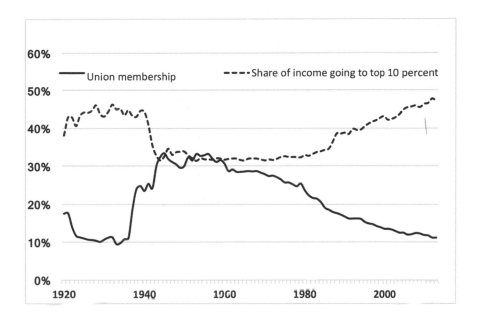

Figure 4.1. Income Inequality and Union Membership. *Source:* **Will Kimball and Lawrence Mishel, "Unions' Decline and the Rise of the Top 10 Percent's Share of Income," Economic Policy Institute, February 3, 2015, http://www.epi.org/ publication/unions-decline-and-the-rise-of-the-top-10-percents-share-of-income.**

and benefit agreements through the collective bargaining process. In the absence of collective bargaining, employees have little or no leverage when it comes to establishing compensation for their labor. A strong labor union presence means more power for workers, higher wages, more generous benefits, and greater equality in the workplace. In addition, economists have also shown that collective bargaining will sometimes raise wages in the nonunion sector, as employers take steps to prevent union expansion by improving working conditions in their companies. This is the threat effect that occurs when union success forces employers to take defensive actions. Labor leaders know that union organizing is most successful under conditions of absolute and relative deprivation, and business leaders know that satisfied workers are less likely to organize a union.

But this is only part of the story; there is another explanation for the impact that unions have on wage equality. This additional explanation considers the indirect effect that labor power has in advancing a moral economy. According to sociologists Bruce Western and Jake Rosenfeld, "the moral economy consists of norms prescribing fair distribution that are institutionalized in the market's formal rules and customs."[6] This is the cultural side of the economy that goes beyond supply/demand ratios and rational calculations of profit and loss.

Edward F. Fischer, an anthropologist who has conducted cross-cultural fieldwork comparing different moral economies, notes: "Economic systems aggressively promote moral values. Economies are evolving historical systems, and moral values are part and parcel of their normal functioning. . . . The ethics of the economy are formed from the ground up in an ongoing creative process, and market values are tightly linked to identity politics and moral discourses around fairness and dignity."[7] Put another way, the moral economy establishes rules for ethical behavior and enforces standards of right and wrong. When the moral economy is healthy, individuals, businesses, and governments that violate cultural expectations of fairness can become the target of vigorous public criticism.

Western and Rosenfeld argue that unions are instrumental in establishing, supporting, and growing a moral economy. Unions do this by advocating publicly for economic equality, by shaping more egalitarian social policy, and by influencing rules that govern the labor market. Unions also institutionalize elements of democracy by giving workers a greater voice in the workplace and by harnessing political influence at both the local and national levels. And unions sustain identities that encourage and empower individuals to participate with confidence in the public sphere, where debate and discourse contributes to a vibrant moral economy.

Under conditions of a robust moral economy, union success is contagious in that the gains of collective bargaining start to spread to nonunion workplaces. Moreover, the positive impact of fairness norms is said to be in addition to wage increases that are given by employers who are simply striving to prevent union organizing. I will not review here the complex statistical modeling employed by Western and Rosenfeld; suffice it to say that they offer compelling evidence that unions do in fact have an indirect social impact on wages throughout the economy. As union influence began to decline in the 1960s, the moral economy was also weakened, which meant that the amoral "logic of the market" could more easily be used to justify wage inequality. Between 1973 and

2007, union membership in the private sector experienced an unprecedented drop from 34 percent to 8 percent for men, and from 16 percent to 6 percent for women. During this same period there was a 40 percent increase in wage inequality. Of course, the dwindling number of private sector unions and the associated weakening of the moral economy is not the only cause of the growing divide between the rich and poor, but the empirical evidence suggests that it is certainly a significant contributing factor.

In the following section, I will continue with the example of labor unions and show how identity at the level of culture operates as a resource in the moral economy and provides a valuable weapon in the fight for dignity and justice in the workplace. This will be followed by a more general discussion of identity, culture, and resistance outside of the labor movement.

RESISTING INEQUALITY AT THE LEVEL OF CULTURE

The success and failure of the labor movement offers a good example of how identity processes operating at the level of culture can serve as a resource for resisting and reforming economic inequality. Union power and influence begin with worker solidarity. Individual employees may have grievances and may experience deprivation, but no single person has the power to alter inequality or advance a moral economy. However, when workers join together and act in concert, their power grows, and positive social change becomes a possibility. The formula is simple: The greater the number of workers acting in solidarity, the stronger the union, and the greater the number of unions, the stronger the moral economy.

The creation of worker solidarity for the purpose of social change depends upon the emergence of a particular type of group, a particular type of group culture, and particular types of identities. The most basic prerequisite is that workers who experience deprivation must move from an attitude of "I" (I am being deprived) to an attitude of "we" (all of us are being deprived) before they can effectively forge collective action. When group solidarity is strong, common cause is realized, and harm to one member is experienced as harm to all members. Under these circumstances, the group will be motivated to take collective action, and individual group members will more likely develop a collective identity.

All of us have multiple identities that define who we are and combine to give us an overall sense of self. Many of these identities represent different groups or categories that we belong to or are a part of— families, religions, political parties, fan clubs, nations, schools, and so forth—but most of these identities are not considered collective identities. A collective identity is unique in that it takes shape in groups that have both a high degree of solidarity and a commitment to collective action for the purpose of social change. A tightly knit family, a network of close friends, and a military combat unit are examples of groups in which people are expected to defend each other's interests and make heroic sacrifices for each other, but identities derived from these groups would not be considered collective identities because they do not normally have a group culture focused on social change. On the other hand, a labor union is a group that is intentionally organized for social change, and it is therefore more likely to be the basis of a collective identity. But even unions may fail to serve as a foundation for collective identity if member solidarity is weak and the group culture does not focus on social activism, social change, or resistance to oppression and deprivation.

Group culture is not always easy to identify, and solidarity can be especially difficult to detect. Because of this, collective acts of resistance often seem spontaneous when sparked by what appears to be a small, inconsequential incident that amounts to the proverbial "last straw on a camel's back." But in fact, sociologist Rick Fantasia found that even spur-of-the-moment acts of resistance are products of a culture of solidarity.[8] Fantasia uses the example of two wildcat strikes that erupted at an iron foundry where he worked—first as a furnace operator and later at various jobs in the finishing department. A wildcat strike is an "unauthorized" refusal to work that is neither sanctioned nor planned by a labor union. It occurs outside of the formal procedures defined in a collective bargaining agreement, and it violates federal labor laws that govern when unions are allowed to "legally strike."

In the first instance described by Fantasia, workers at the foundry walked off the job when a likable coworker was fired for falling asleep during his shift. In the second instance, workers shut down the factory to protest the lack of heat in the company break room. Both actions were successful in that the coworker retained his job and the company decided to heat the break room. But both actions were also highly risky. If only a handful of workers walked out, the strikers would be immediately fired and replaced. Success required that all workers act in unison at almost exactly the same time. Fantasia found that a culture of solidarity was not automatically available but had to be created in the moment:

> The solidarity the strike achieved and expressed was not inherent in the workforce, as some might romantically contend, but was to a significant degree a product of the collective action itself. But although solidarity was not an a priori "fact," neither was it without a social basis. For the conditions of the work and the day-to-day social interaction they shaped created at least a surface level of mutuality, a foundation of trust among the workers.[9]

Thus, even though a collective identity presupposes group solidarity and a group culture, the process is not necessarily linear and sequential. Mutual trust and interpersonal relationships can serve as the foundation for "spontaneous" acts of collective resistance, which in turn contribute to the development of cultures of solidarity.

When workers take part in a wildcat strike and intentionally disrupt the routine pattern of labor relations, they are simultaneously engaged in two different types of resistance—one material and the other symbolic. In the first type, they are trying to secure a larger share of the company profits and a work environment that is more humane and less physically oppressive. We see this expressed in the battle over wages, benefits, and working conditions. This is for the most part a struggle over the material world, and it is reflected in questions such as "How should available material resources be distributed?" and "Who has the power to physically control the distribution of material resources?"

The second type of resistance is less obvious in that it represents a struggle over dignity, respect, and identity meanings. Here the battle is cultural and symbolic, and it is represented in questions such as "What does it mean to be a worker?" and "How much value and power should be attached to the worker identity?" This type of resistance is less about the distribution of material resources and more about the value and power of an identity. When a labor union realizes a high degree of solidarity, and when a collective identity is firmly established, group members will not only hold each other in high regard, but they will also experience a shared sense of power. Under these conditions, the meaning of the worker identity is essentially transformed within the culture of the group. The dominant identity interpretations established by the employer are replaced by new meanings that emerge from the bottom up.

Without a union and absent a collective identity, workers not only have less power to secure material resources, but they also experience less respect, less deference, and less dignity. In situations such as these, the worker identity is largely defined by the company culture and usually from the top down—a power play that deprives the self of personal autonomy, the experience of agency, and a sense of authenticity.

The main point I want to make here is that identity meanings at the level of culture can vary between groups, and as we saw in chapter 2, these meanings can range from the highly positive to the highly negative. Dominant groups have the ability to impose their own cultural interpretations of an identity on the dominated. Resistance at the level of culture occurs when less dominant groups object to negative cultural interpretations of an identity and work to create their own, more positive, meanings. In the case of workers who organize a union, this means that union members will work to advance their own identity interpretations in opposition to the identity meanings advocated by company managers and owners. While the competition between workers and their employers is fundamentally a struggle over the control and distribution of material resources (e.g., wages, benefits, and working conditions), it is important to recognize that this competition is simultaneously a struggle over the control of cultural resources (i.e., identity meanings). This is a distinction that parallels the difference between the material economy and the moral economy discussed above. When unions are strong, the union identity will be viewed in more positive terms and be more highly valued in the larger culture. But when unions are weak, negative interpretations of the identity will prevail and the identity will be devalued in the larger culture.

Transforming Identity Meanings at the Level of Culture

Small gatherings of people who voluntarily meet on a regular basis for a common purpose (as in the union example) are more likely to have overlapping identity meanings that are relatively specific. In this context it is not surprising to find group solidarity. Members of a small group tend to have personal connections with each other and a greater sense of loyalty. But the farther removed one gets from a small-group setting, the less precise any shared meanings become, and face-to-face interactions, mutual experiences, and common stories become fewer and farther between. Workers on the day shift of the factory floor, for instance, have less in common with the workers on the swing shift, and workers at another company factory in a different city have less in common still. Not only is solidarity more difficult to achieve in larger groups, but it is also true that the development of a collective identity becomes especially challenging. This poses obvious problems for individuals and groups that want to resist inequality on a national or international scale. But even here, successful resistance is possible.

Consider, for example, the case of gay rights in the United States. In a period of less than fifty years, gay men and lesbians were able to achieve historic advances toward liberation, including the repeal of sodomy laws, the removal of homosexuality from lists of mental disorders, the institution of legal protections in the workplace, and the right to marry and adopt children. Along the way, the public's attitude toward gay people has undergone a correspondingly dramatic shift. For example, in 1973 when a representative sample of US adults was asked whether "sexual relations between two adults of the same sex is always wrong, almost always wrong, wrong only sometimes, or not wrong at all," a large majority of respondents (70 percent) said "always wrong" and only 11 percent stated "not wrong at all." However, by the year 2012, the US population was evenly split on the issue, with less than half of the respondents saying "always wrong" (43 percent), and nearly as many saying "not wrong at all" (42 percent).[10]

This striking swing in social policy and public beliefs about sexual relations is the result of a powerful social movement built around a collective identity. It is an especially noteworthy transformation from a sociological perspective because of the speed and scope of the change. In fact, according to historian John D'Emilio, homosexual desire did not even develop into a recognizable identity category in American culture until the second half of the nineteenth century: "Only when individuals began to make their living through wage labor, instead of as parts of an interdependent family unit, was it possible for homosexual desire to coalesce into a personal identity—an identity based on the ability to remain outside the heterosexual family and to construct a personal life based on attraction to one's own sex."[11]

This is not to say that men and women did not experience an erotic attraction to their own sex in the preindustrial era; same-sex desire certainly existed at this time. However homosexual desire and behavior did not form a recognizable identity—one could not live one's life as a "homosexual" or as a "lesbian"—and others would not legitimate such an identity claim in everyday encounters.[12] Before an individual can claim a personal identity, the identity must first be recognized and validated within a larger group. And before a group identity can become a collective identity, group members must experience solidarity over shared grievances. This presupposes the existence of a "gay community."

Prior to World War II, a visible urban subculture of gay men and lesbians did not exist in the United States. The war, however, disrupted and transformed traditional work and family relationships for millions of young people, and it restructured the location and manner in which young people encountered each other. For men, the war institutionalized same-sex living in military barracks and facilitated the emergence of a unique form of male solidarity. For women, the war was also transformative. New employment opportunities allowed women to leave the family home for work in the cities, where many were housed in same-sex rooming houses. With new forms of independence, new experiences, and new opportunities, the first gay communities gradually emerged during the 1950s and 1960s, and for the first time in US history, a distinct gay identity was socially recognized and accepted by some. This was evidenced in the growth of gay literary societies, novels with gay characters, news stories about gay people, and social gathering spaces in the form of bathhouses, bars, and social clubs—all rare or nonexistent a century earlier.

But this new visibility also instigated a backlash by the medical establishment, religious institutions, and the state. The formation of new communities and new identities can threaten and disrupt the traditional social order, instigating a defensive response by dominant institutions. During the 1950s the American Psychiatric Association listed homosexuality as a "sociopathic personality disturbance" in need of a cure. In the labor market, many gay men and lesbians were identified as "perverts" or security threats and were fired from government jobs, including the military. Domination and discrimination were also evident in the private life of gay people as vice squads regularly raided gay bars and other meeting places.

Yet, in an ironic sociological twist, the institutionalized discrimination and oppression that occurred throughout the 1950s and 1960s actually served to enhance solidarity among individuals with a burgeoning gay identity. Heightened repression validated grievances, reinforced the desire for liberation, and fueled a motivation to act. Collective frustration with public harassment reached a tipping point in 1969 when a police raid provoked an uprising outside of a gay bar in Manhattan. The so-called Stonewall Riot (after the name of the bar) lasted for several days, attracted thousands of supporters, and served as the defining event in the emergence of the modern gay rights movement. With an established network of social relationships in place and a critical mass of individuals claiming a gay identity, the conditions were ripe for the formation of a social movement and the emergence of a collective identity defined by sexual orientation.

Unlike the labor movement, the gay liberation movement is not explicitly defined by the unequal distribution of material resources. Some gay men, lesbians, bisexuals, and transgendered persons certainly experience economic exploitation, but this is not the primary issue of concern as it is in the labor movement. Rather, gay rights organizations, such as the Human Rights Campaign, are more generally focused on changing the dominant cultural meanings associated with gay identities, so that "lesbian, gay, bisexual and transgender people are embraced as full members of society at home, at work and in every community."[13] While the general public attends mostly to the political struggle that is being waged for equal rights under the law, the more fundamental skirmish in the movement is over symbolic boundaries that mark the dominant cultural interpretations of an identity.

Identity boundary work in a social movement must often reconcile two somewhat opposing objectives: (1) to redefine a devalued identity as "normal" so as to achieve inclusion and acceptance in the dominant culture, and (2) to clarify, reinforce, and expand a distinct collective identity so as to facilitate the mobilization of a large number of activists. For example, in appropriating the term "queer," gay activists have sought to construct a more inclusive identity of people with a wide range of sexualities. But this diversity and distinctiveness within the movement (visually displayed at many Gay Pride parades) can work against acceptance and inclusion outside the movement. Assimilation into a dominant culture is easier when gay/queer people look, sound, and act like "normal people." But this type of conformity can erect boundaries within the oppressed group, creating internal strife and limiting solidarity. Sociologist Joshua Gamson, for example, found that the representation of gay people on television served to normalize and legitimate middle-class gay people while simultaneously invalidating the identities of poor and working-class gays. [14]

Resistance at the level of culture occurs when devalued and powerless identity meanings are contested and revised. It is evident in the so-called culture wars that are waged between groups defending "traditional" social practices and those advocating for a more inclusive and less discriminatory way of life. [15] This is never an easy transformation, and it usually takes decades of struggle. Success at this level requires the collective mobilization of people who share an identity, the development of group solidarity, and the emergence of collective identities. While many of these battles are fought in the media, in legislative bodies, and at the ballot box, macro-level shifts in identity meaning also depend on resistance in everyday face-to-face encounters.

RESISTING INEQUALITY AT THE LEVEL OF INTERACTION

Resistance at the level of interaction occurs in specific social situations where two or more people are engaged in face-to-face contact. In normal circumstances, such encounters follow a predictable and recognizable script in which actors use identity categories to determine socially expected displays of deference and demeanor. For this reason, deference and demeanor may appear to be nothing more than "good manners" or customary etiquette. But beneath the surface of everyday interaction lies a system of social control where value and power are linked to specific identities defined by relationships of domination and subordination. Resistance, therefore, occurs when established rules of interaction are ignored, challenged, or rejected.

We were all born into a world in which patterns of unequal deference and dominance were already firmly established. As a consequence, we learn to expect and to accept an unjust interaction order at a very early age. For sociologist Erving Goffman, inequality at the level of interaction is also perpetuated by an implicit threat against those who would resist: "Behind a willingness to accept the way things are ordered is the brutal fact of one's place in the social structure and the real or imagined cost of allowing oneself to be singled out as a malcontent." To be "singled out" is to be excluded from the group; it means a new identity as a "malcontent," "deviant," or "troublemaker" along with the uncomfortable meanings associated with such categories. For this reason, Goffman observes that "categories of individual in every time and place have exhibited a disheartening capacity for overtly accepting miserable interactional arrangements."[16]

While our capacity to accept "miserable interactional arrangements" is indeed pervasive and disheartening, resistance and defiance at the level of interaction are not uncommon. Indeed, most of us have likely engaged in some form of identity resistance at the level of interaction at some point in our lives. Consider, for example, the times when you felt disrespected, ignored, or exploited and you objected, spoke up, or complained. These may be remembered as tense, emotional confrontations, but there is a good chance that they were also moments of resistance to the experience of inequality. For many of us, these episodes are found in our employment history and our worker identity.

Workplace Defiance at the Level of Interaction

For several summers during my youth I worked at a blueberry farm with other teens. We picked berries for a piece rate—the more berries I picked the more I was paid. Most of us would earn less than the minimum wage after toiling away for eight hours a day in the summer heat. However, if you were deemed a "good worker" and had enough seniority, you might be moved to the sorting belt where employees were paid by the hour and worked in the shade of the sorting shed. During my second season at the farm I was offered a position as a sorter, and I was delighted! No more sweltering heat, a guaranteed wage, and a more enjoyable work experience—or so I thought. My new job was simple: Stand in front of a moving conveyor belt covered with blueberries and remove any "imperfections." Green berries, stems, and leaves were considered imperfections. My first day went well. It took me a few hours to learn the technique and achieve the speed of the more experienced sorters, but by the end of the day I was keeping pace with the belt. But things went downhill after that.

Halfway through my shift on the second day I was ready to quit. The challenge of learning a new job was gone, and the monotony of the task was starting to play tricks on my mind. I was having trouble with my concentration as I found myself hypnotized by the river of blue passing in front of me. If I looked away, I would miss imperfections, but if I kept my eyes fixed and uninterrupted on the belt, I would slowly begin to hallucinate. Berries began changing colors before my eyes; green berries turned into blueberries and blueberries turned green. The only relief came when a mechanical failure jammed the belt or a worker who fell behind was forced to push the stop button.

Pushing the stop button was a serious offense. A loud horn would sound, supervisors would scramble, and all eyes would turn to locate the guilty worker. If one employee were identified as a regular "belt stopper," he or she would be reprimanded or sent back to the field. On my second day, I was on the verge of becoming a regular belt stopper. I had little choice: either stop the belt and save my sanity, or remain in a trance and be disciplined for missing the imperfections. Either way, I was at risk of losing my job. Although I did stop the belt a couple of times over the eight-hour shift, at the end of the day I was still employed. I was saved by the fact that the belt was randomly stopped about once every hour, and almost always at the exact time when I was most desperate for a break. Sometimes another sorter would fall behind and stop the line, and other times the belt would simply malfunction. I wasn't sure I would be so lucky on day three.

On my third day as a blueberry sorter I discovered a little secret that saved my job and preserved my sanity. It turned out that the intermittent belt stopping that I experienced on day two was not as random as I had originally thought. In conversation with the more experienced employees I learned that they too suffered from similar delusions and hypnotic episodes, but behind the backs of the supervisors they had developed a strategy whereby workers would take turns stopping the belt. By distributing the "violation" evenly across the line, no one person would be consistently singled out. I also learned that many of the mechanical breakdowns weren't technically "accidents." The farm bosses were unaware of the fact that some of the more skilled belt workers were intentionally sabotaging the machinery. Over the next few days I was slowly integrated into the belt disruption scheme as I learned how to look the other way when the machinery was purposely jammed, and on cue I took my turn stopping the belt. It was a lesson that served me well for more than a decade as I moved from one temporary or part-time job to another.

For instance, I discovered almost identical disruption strategies while employed at a Weyerhaeuser mill where I pulled lumber off a continuously running "green chain." Jamming and line stoppage were also commonly used to slow down the pace of work at United Parcel Service, where I sorted packages on an incessantly moving conveyor belt. And I participated in similar slowdown strategies while working a drill press at an industrial machine shop one summer.

In all of these jobs, I joined with my fellow employees to limit the control of a demanding employer, slow an unrelenting machine, relieve monotony, and reclaim a bit of dignity. This is a form of covert or "hidden resistance" in that supervisors were mostly unaware of the organized and intentional foot-dragging. Secret acts of sabotage, anonymous trickery, and behind-the-back grumbling have long been used by exploited groups of people struggling under oppressive conditions and close supervision. These tactics have persisted for centuries because they provide relief from punishing mental and physical labor, and they reflect an underground struggle for power. Indeed, political scientist James C. Scott has argued that "most of the political life of subordinate groups is to be found neither in overt collective defiance of power holders nor in complete hegemonic compliance, but in the vast territory between these two polar opposites." [17]

Sociologist Randy Hodson conducted a comprehensive review of over eighty different ethnographic studies of the workplace, and produced a catalog of the many different acts of defiance on the part of employees. [18] In his analysis of these cases, he found four distinct strategies for coping with indignities: resistance, citizenship, the creation of independent meaning systems, and the development of social relations at work. As used by Hodson, resistance encompasses destructive acts, sabotage, theft, foot-dragging, and the withdrawal of cooperation. Citizenship refers to actions that are intended to enhance self-worth despite the indignities of the immediate context. These are enterprising activities that serve as alternative sources of pride—doing a job well, perfecting a skill—and are largely independent of the formal demands of power. Autonomous meaning systems also emerge among workers who seek value, purpose, and control within an overarching system of supervision and management. This can involve personal rituals or the display of symbols that represent life outside of the workplace. Examples include engaging in games during lunch breaks, joking with coworkers, or personalizing a workspace by exhibiting family photos, sport memorabilia, or hobby emblems. Finally, fundamental to all of these strategies is coworker relations—where collective identity is formed separate from management. Here informal ties and patterns of mutual assistance can develop into unofficial work site roles and identities. When group values and leadership positions emerge from coworker relations, a united opposition to oppressive conditions is possible.

Other ethnographic studies have documented similar acts of collective resistance in schools and neighborhoods.[19] In all of these accounts we find rich descriptions of situated resistance that often occurs behind the backs of the powerful, inside commanding institutional structures, and against the interests of state and market forces.

While acts of underground resistance may be vast, this form of opposition only rarely alters the structures of inequality and has relatively little effect on the identity meanings of employer and employee. The secrecy and subtlety of the resistance does little to challenge the power of a dominant group. Nevertheless, over time, an accumulation of indignities may create enough pressure to break the wall of silence. When the private becomes public, identity meanings are openly contested in face-to-face interaction where established rules of deference are disrupted.

Consider, for example, the following exchange reported by sociologist Anna Pollert in her ethnography of women factory workers in Bristol, England. Here, a company manager (Mr. Dowling) is publicly challenged by one of the line workers (Ivy):

> Ivy: Where are you going for your holidays this year, Mr. Dowling?
>
> Mr. Dowling: I'm not going anywhere. I can't afford it. I bought the wife a car and I've spent our money. Honestly.
>
> Ivy: Have you? Ah! What a shame. Can't you sell some of your shares then?

Mr. Dowling: No, can't do that.

Ivy: Come on, just a few.

This produced laughter all round, the manager and his attempt at being "just one of the workers" exposed to ridicule, and at the same time exploited for a laugh.[20]

While the exchange is brief and subtle, it serves as an unmistakable affront to the legitimacy of Mr. Dowling's authority. Not only is Mr. Dowling teased and "knocked down a peg," but his higher income and class position are also the source of the humor. The playful act of resistance is enabled by the nature of the setting: a factory manager visiting workers in their territory on the factory floor. One can imagine that if a similar conversation had occurred in Mr. Dowling's office, where Ivy was without an audience of supportive colleagues, the interpretation would be quite different. Here, the public nature of the interaction allows for the expression of worker solidarity and creates a temporary shift in power. For a brief moment, Mr. Dowling was no longer in control, and the women were able to assert a degree of independence from the factory rules and formal status hierarchy.

When a dominant interaction order is regularly disrupted by a series of public challenges over a period of time, identity meanings will gradually change. In a workplace environment, this could mean an increase in the power and value of a worker identity and a leveling of the authority structure. In most cases, however, resistance at the level of interaction will provoke a reactionary response on the part of management in an attempt to control the definition of the situation from the top down. This could mean a renewed emphasis on employee "trainings," the imposition of disciplinary actions, or the firing of identifiable "troublemakers." For this reason, most resistance at the level of interaction remains discreet, restrained, and underground.

There are, however, moments in history when resistance at the level of interaction is so effective that it contributes to the transformation of society. We see this in the civil rights movement that emerged in response to the oppressive system of racial segregation and discrimination in American society.

Social Etiquette, Domination, and Black Resistance

Economists Lee Alston and Joseph Ferrie suggest that a paternalistic system of deference and social etiquette between blacks and whites in the South following the Civil War was critical to the maintenance of the new agricultural economy. Former slaves and their descendants had greater economic freedom following emancipation, but their options were narrowly confined. White farmers, on the other hand, needed agricultural workers to maintain the plantations but they could no longer command employment from the former slaves.[21] As a solution, former slaveholders induced some blacks to stay on the plantations as tenant farmers by offering benefits such as housing, firewood, protection from a racist legal system, and a degree of safety from white violence. However, this paternalistic relationship was strictly maintained with a demanding system of deference and appropriate demeanor. African Americans may have been freed from the bondage of slavery but they were not free of the rules of domination and subordination that characterized black-white social relations. The new economic system called for new rules of racial etiquette in order to control the newly empowered black identities that were developing during the period of Reconstruction.

Historian J. William Harris notes that some of the rules of etiquette were codified into law, while others were grounded in local knowledge and varied from place to place.[22] A black man, for example, was expected to remove his hat (or at least bow while touching the hat) when greeting a white man, but white men would be chastened if they displayed the same deference to a black man. White men, on the other hand, were expected to remove their hat when greeting a white woman, but would not do so in conversation with a black woman. Similarly, black people were required to use formal titles when addressing whites (Sir, Mister, Missus, or Boss) but white people would employ only first names, intentionally avoiding the use of honorary titles and the respect that they engender. For black men, the derogatory "boy" was a common form of address, along with "darky," "colored person," and "nigger," and for black women, "girl," "auntie," or "wench" were regularly employed.

To be identified as a "negro" meant you were "simple-minded," "not fully human," and "not capable of self-control." But for most whites, blackness also connoted something much deeper and more fundamental. From the perspective of the dominant white culture, blackness was also considered impure, spoiled, and polluted. The "negro" was not only a degraded identity, but it was also potentially dangerous. For this reason, the boundaries between black and white were regularly patrolled and guarded lest white purity be defiled by inappropriate contact with the impure.[23]

With the sudden freeing of the slaves, not only was the old economic order destroyed, but the interactional order was also in jeopardy. By formalizing the rules of racial etiquette, white racists were reasserting and reaffirming the superiority of their white racial identity while, at the same time, reinforcing the walls separating the pure from the impure, the clean from the dirty, and the safe from the dangerous. These boundaries were deemed especially necessary in public places where the old interaction order was most precarious and equal contact was most threatening. What was "naturalized" under slavery was now "institutionalized" under Jim Crow with signs, statutes, codes, and regulations that applied to parks, movie theaters, hotels, hospitals, buses, trains, streetcars, schools, libraries, civic organizations, and business establishments of all kinds.

Because racial etiquette was so critical for the maintenance of a racial hierarchy, breaking etiquette and resisting expected rituals of deference in public settings was considered a serious offense that would often provoke harsh and sometimes deadly retribution. At stake were not simply the appropriate manners of a "good negro," but a system of privilege and dominance that defined the larger moral and social order. Writing in 1928, sociologist Robert Park recognized this larger context: "This is the significance of the ceremonial and social ritual so rigidly enforced in the South, by which racial distinctions are preserved amid all the inevitable changes and promiscuity of an expanding industrial and democratic society. While etiquette and ceremonial ritual are at once convenience and a necessity in facilitating human intercourse, they serve even more effectively to preserve rank and order of individuals and classes, which seems to be essential to social organization and effective collective action."[24]

Understanding the sociological significance of racial etiquette allows for a deeper appreciation of the power of civil disobedience. When Rosa Parks refused to relinquish her bus seat to a white person on that fateful evening in 1955, she was not simply breaking the law in Mont-

gomery, Alabama, but she was also ignoring the rules of etiquette regarding public transportation. And in the process, she was disrupting an
established interaction order that both offended and frightened white
citizens. Rosa Parks knew that she was insulting white passengers, she
knew that she would be arrested for breaking the law, but more important, she also understood the power embedded in the symbolism of her
act. Her defiance was monumental not simply because she violated a
city ordinance that become a test case for the courts. Her refusal to
follow white etiquette became a historical milestone because her resistance was intentionally linked to a chain of events strategically designed
to alter the interaction order. The bus boycott and legal challenges that
followed helped to change the political and legal landscape, but integrated seating also began the slow revolution toward a more egalitarian
system of deference and demeanor where racial power and privilege is
not reproduced and legitimated in the subtleties of everyday etiquette.

All of us have at least a tacit understanding of the power and symbolic significance of an established interaction order. We may not be able
to describe or articulate its precise workings, but we are immediately
aware of those instances when interpersonal rules and expectations are
violated. When common discourtesies and faux pas are intentionally
organized and sustained over a period of time, the offense is especially
noticeable and threatening to the dominant order. For this reason, the
reaction of those in power is typically emotional and can provoke a
defensive response that is quite often fierce and violent. This is poignantly illustrated in the following account provided by Ann Moody, a
young African American activist who violated the expectation that white
and black people were not to dine together on equal terms in the same
restaurant. Along with other civil rights activists, she deliberately ignored social etiquette by taking a seat at a Woolworth's lunch counter in
Jackson, Mississippi.

> "Which one should I get first?" a big husky boy said. "That white
> nigger," the old man said. The boy lifted Joan from the counter by
> her waist and carried her outside the store. Simultaneously I was
> snatched from my stool by two high school students. I was dragged
> about thirty feet toward the door by my hair when someone made
> them turn me loose. As I was getting up off the floor, I saw Joan
> coming back inside. We started back to the center of the counter to
> join Pearlina. Lois Chaffee, a white Tougaloo faculty member, was

now sitting next to her. So Joan and I just climbed across the rope at the front end of the counter and sat down. There were now four of us, two whites and two Negroes, all women. The mob started smearing us with ketchup, mustard, sugar, pies, and everything on the counter. Soon Joan and I were joined by John Salter, but the moment he sat down he was hit on the jaw with what appeared to be brass knuckles. Blood gushed from his face and someone threw salt into the open wound.[25]

This intentional provocation was one of a series of related sit-ins organized throughout the South. In most instances, hostile white patrons reacted with similar rage and fury. From an outsider's perspective, the aggressive community response is difficult to comprehend. The sit-in appears to be a rather minor offense; the presence of an African American at a lunch counter does not seem to harm white customers and does not appear to interfere with white business. Indeed, one could even argue that if African Americans were allowed to eat at the counter, it would mean more customers, which, at least theoretically, should be good for business. But small acts of resistance at the level of interaction can trigger intense emotions because the stability and security of an established self is often jeopardized.

In 1960, many white southerners experienced the sit-ins as a personal affront to the power and privilege of their white identity. They may not have been able to explain their vociferous reactions, but they could feel their repulsion to equality, and they feared the crumbling of a stable interaction order. With each sit-in and with each integrated restaurant, school, and bus, one more brick was being dislodged from the foundation of white power and privilege. When an established interaction order begins to collapse, shock waves from the demolition are felt at both the level of culture, where established identity meanings are disrupted, and at the person level, where an individual's sense of self may also be dislodged. In the following section I will take a closer look at identity and resistance at the person level and explore how changing identity meanings may also serve as a powerful resource in the production of a more egalitarian society.

RESISTING INEQUALITY AT THE PERSON LEVEL

When an identity category is devalued in a culture, and when everyday interaction reinforces the relative powerlessness of the same identity, the self is subjugated and injured. Outsiders are mostly unaware of the wounds of identity inequality. They cannot see the damage inflicted when dignity is denied, or feel the pain of recurring disrespect and disregard. For this reason, complaints about harm are often ignored, diminished, or dismissed as an "overreaction."

Resistance at the person level occurs when an individual reacts to an assault on the self and pushes back against an oppressive social structure. Sometimes the resistance is disorganized, ineffective, or misplaced, and it does little to alter the system of inequality. Other times, however, the self is transformed into an agent of change where new activist identities serve as resources for reform and revolution. In this section I will explore examples of both types of resistance. I begin with a brief discussion of the link between inequality and the personal experience of disrespect.

Disrespect

One need not have a sophisticated philosophical understanding of justice to know when an injustice has occurred. All of us possess an intuitive capacity to recognize when we have been treated unfairly, when we have been denied the recognition that we feel we deserve, and when our dignity and honor have been maligned. A healthy, flourishing self depends upon stable social relationships, and no personal identity can thrive without positive social recognition. This fact has led philosopher Axel Honneth to argue rather convincingly that the negative experience of disrespect is key to understanding the connection between individual identity and societal systems of inequality:

> The criterion now becomes the intersubjective condition of human identity development. The conditions can be found in social forms of communication in which the individual grows up, acquires a social identity and ultimately has to learn to conceive of him or herself as both an equal and unique member of society. If these forms of communication do not provide the amount of recognition necessary to accomplish the various tasks involved in forming an identity, then

this must be taken as an indication of a society's pathological development.[26]

According to Honneth, social relationships and social institutions that
limit social recognition and constrain access to valued identities are not
only "pathological," but the disrespect that they engender constitutes a
"moral injury." Whereas a physical injury wounds the body, a moral
injury wounds the self. Economic exploitation can mean hunger, disease, and exposure to extreme heat and cold, but it also means a loss of
esteem, humiliation, and the denial of dignity. We should not forget
that human suffering has both a physical side and a moral side. A suffering body means a suffering self, and a disrespected self will necessarily
produce a suffering body.

The relationship between moral and physical injury is well illustrated
in sociologist Elijah Anderson's ethnographic study of poverty and violence in what he describes as a "ghetto" neighborhood of Philadelphia.
Anderson's research describes the personal and interpersonal consequences of an economic and judicial system that has failed inner-city
African American families. In this sociological context, the code of the
street has emerged as the dominant normative system for negotiating
daily life. It is, in essence, a set of informal rules for regulating public
behavior, especially with regard to violence. "At the heart of the code is
the issue of respect—loosely defined as being treated 'right' or being
granted one's 'props' (or proper due) or the deference one deserves."[27]

When social institutions have been structured in such a way that
they disadvantage a particular category of people, respect is experienced as a scarce resource that is often protected and defended with
ferocity:

> In the street culture, especially among young people, respect is
> viewed as almost an external entity, one that is hard-won but easily
> lost—and so must constantly be guarded. The rules of the code in
> fact provide a framework for negotiating respect. With the right
> amount of respect, individuals can avoid being bothered in public.
> This security is important, for if they are bothered, not only may they
> face physical danger, but they will have been disgraced or "dissed"
> (disrespected).[28]

In this context, the physical suffering of poverty is associated with the moral injury of being disrespected (generally speaking), and because respect is so tenuous for those living in poverty, to "diss" someone risks provoking a physical confrontation. In other words, physical injury invites moral injury, and moral injury invites physical injury in a continuous cycle of harm to both the body and the self.

Outsiders who are not governed by the code of the street might struggle to understand how minor insults can have such catastrophic consequences. Some might even question the veracity of Anderson's research. But those with an intimate understanding of violent crime in the United States know that an argument or disagreement can have lethal consequences if it leads to humiliation and the experience of disrespect.[29] To illustrate this point I have reproduced below a sample of recent news headlines from US cities, where "disrespect" was associated with a homicide.

> Prosecutors: Man killed two who "disrespected" his dad on July 4 (May 13, 2015, *Chicago Tribune*)
>
> Ex-con gets 247 years for killing man who "disrespected" girlfriend (November 6, 2015, FOX 5 San Diego)
>
> Prosecutor: Man shot in East Oakland drug house over perceived disrespect (June 30, 2014, CBS SF Bay Area)
>
> Burien man claims he shot to death Shell employee because of disrespect (August 21, 2014, *Kent Reporter*)
>
> Disrespect motivated Fat Kat nightclub shooting (September 5, 2014, WOKV Jacksonville)
>
> Meier allegedly shot Mende due to "disrespect," tried to get friends to take blame for murder (February 21, 2014, iFIBER News)
>
> Anchorage police: Fatal shooting followed perceived disrespect (February 16, 2015, *Alaska Dispatch News*)
>
> Threat or disrespect? Florida loud music trial begins (February 16, 2014, CBS News Online)
>
> Jurors told disrespect led to 2013 Greensboro homicide (March 19, 2015, *Greensboro News and Record*)
>
> Disrespect: Guns, teens, and death in Wilmington (February 7, 2015, *News Journal*)
>
> Killings over "respect" are frequent in Birmingham (June 5, 2015, Yellowhammer Multimedia, Birmingham, Alabama)

Killing another person because one has been "disrespected" may seem like an enormously disproportionate response, but when someone has few claims to esteem, a public humiliation can be experienced as an ultimate indignity that calls for an ultimate rejoinder. Murder is not only the most extreme form of physical violence; it is also the final assault on another person's selfhood and dignity.

Interpersonal violence is one consequence of inequality. When the self is deprived of recognition, respect, and dignity, a person's reaction may be defensive, emotional, and aggressive. In this context, some physical assaults, even murder, can be interpreted as a defensive response and a form of resistance to inequality. It is an ineffective and misplaced form of resistance, to be sure, and from an objective sociological perspective we can see that it does not advance equality. But we should not forget that identity is constructed, contested, and defended in everyday face-to-face encounters. For young people in impoverished inner-city neighborhoods, these everyday encounters on the city sidewalks, in the school hallways, at the bus stops, and at the local convenience stores are framed by the code of the street and the threat of violence. Understanding this context is important. Once again, Elijah Anderson:

> Their very identity, their self-respect, and their honor are often intricately tied up with the way they perform on the streets during and after such encounters. And it is this identity, including a credible reputation for payback, or vengeance, that is strongly believed to deter future assaults.[30]

While an aggressive physical response may help deter future assaults—that is, as a form of resistance to oppression—it does not address the social structural foundation of inequality or enhance the power and value of an identity category. In fact, interpersonal violence usually invites a harsh response from law enforcement, and it may also reproduce negative identity meanings associated with class, race, and gender.

Resistance to inequality at the person level will remain ineffective until an assault on one's dignity is confronted collectively and in collaboration with others who experience similar forms of humiliation and disrespect. This, however, requires the development of a collective identity that is internalized as a personally salient part of the self.

Internalizing a Collective Identity

Earlier I argued that inequality could be successfully resisted and re-formed if oppressed people are able to develop a collective identity. A collective identity develops when experiences of deprivation move from an "I" orientation (I am deprived) to a "we" orientation (all of us are deprived). But more important, collective identities go beyond tradi-tional forms of group solidarity and mutual trust to include new identity meanings defined by protest, collective action, and social change.

It is important to understand, however, that not all individuals who claim a collective identity will necessarily share the same degree of devotion and loyalty to the group, or the same measure of commitment to group action and protest. Labor unions, for example, have historically been the basis for collective identity, group protest, and advocacy for greater economic equality, but within the labor movement, the union identity may be more or less salient for individual members. For some people, a family identity, a religious identity, or even an occupational identity may be more important and central to their sense of self than their identity as a union member. We see evidence of this, for example, when a union calls for a strike and some members decide to cross the picket line in defiance of their own collective identity. In this section I want to explore the problem of identity salience in the struggle against inequality.[31] How is it that a collective identity comes to be a prominent feature of the self and a guiding source of motivation and action? Or more precisely, why is it that some people become active and commit-ted participants to a social movement while others do not?

Sociologists Doug McAdam and Ronnelle Paulsen's study of American civil rights activists offers a partial answer to this question.[32] Their retrospective research focused on hundreds of college students who volunteered to participate in the 1964 Mississippi Freedom Sum-mer Project. This was an especially demanding instance of collective action, as well as a historically significant event in the struggle for racial equality. Most project volunteers were harassed, physically assaulted, and arrested during their service, and ten days into the summer-long action, three of the volunteers were kidnapped and murdered by a group of Mississippi segregationists who acted with impunity.

Despite the brutal and sensational attack that took the life of Mickey Schwerner, James Chaney, and Andrew Goodman, the rest of the students continued their work of registering black voters, organizing an alternative political party, and teaching at the newly formed freedom schools. They did so under hazardous social conditions and at great risk of bodily harm. Unlike the black residents of Mississippi who regularly endured racial violence and had few options, the project volunteers were mostly white, economically privileged, and free to return to their northern communities at any time. So why did they stay? What was it about these young students that set them apart from their peers and sustained their commitment to a dangerous collective identity?

McAdam and Paulsen looked for answers to this question in the original interviews and the detailed questionnaires that were completed by students when they initially applied to become a volunteer. The researchers also contacted more than three hundred of the applicants twenty years later with a new questionnaire and additional in-depth interviews. One of the more unique features of these data is that they include information from applicants who were initially accepted but later changed their mind and decided against participating in the Freedom Summer Project. By comparing the volunteers and the "no-shows," McAdam and Paulsen were able to determine critical differences in social background, social relationships, attitudes, and values between participants and nonparticipants.

The most significant finding from this study was that a commitment to Freedom Summer was most likely when a student's participation was linked to an existing identity—such as one's religion, family, education, or civic group. Moreover, what differentiated the volunteers from the no-shows was the amount of support they received from this linkage. To quote McAdam and Paulsen: "Not only were the volunteers embedded in more organizations, but also in ones—civil rights organizations, teacher associations, and so forth—ideally suited to reinforcing the linkage between identity and action."[33]

We are all embedded in multiple social relationships associated with many different identities. While this complex set of meanings may at times be contradictory (e.g., a devout Christian serving as a soldier in a military), we continue to strive for a more or less coherent sense of self, and we expect others to do the same. Because we are motivated to think and act in a consistent way, we must take into consideration our existing identities when faced with the option of taking on a new (collective) identity. It is much easier to become a civil rights activist and to vigorously resist inequality when receiving support from important people in our life. Similarly, we are more likely to receive support from our family, friends, and colleagues when our actions appear consistent with already existing identities. This means that the internalization of a collective identity is not simply an individual or psychological process, but rather, it depends upon our social ties, the cultural meanings associated with our preexisting identities, and the way in which the new collective identity is socially interpreted.

It is also important to recognize that the relative importance or salience of a social movement identity is also determined by social forces outside of a person's own social network. War, booms and busts in the economy, major demographic shifts, disease epidemics, shifts in migration patterns, environmental disruptions, and changes in governmental policy all have the potential to alter regular patterns of interaction, modify social relationships, and simultaneously impact the significance of a given identity. These are the higher-level forces that indirectly shape identity salience from the top down. And because higher-level forces have such a wide impact, they tend to play a prominent role in the emergence of mass protests and the development of social movement organizations. Evidence of this effect was found in a study of Dutch farmers conducted by sociologists Bert Klandermans and Marga de Weerd.[34]

Over a period of three years, Klandermans and de Weerd conducted regular interviews with a sample of 168 Dutch farmers (one interview per farmer per year). Each year the farmers were asked a range of questions designed to measure two things: (1) the relative importance of their farmer identity, and (2) their intention to participate in protest actions against government policy. During this period, Dutch farmers were experiencing declining incomes, cuts to agricultural subsidies, and demanding environmental policies. As a consequence, most farmers felt that the value of the farmer identity was in decline and that they were losing power relative to other occupational groups in society.

Analyses of the interview data showed that the farmers who were most committed to their farmer identity were more likely to engage in protest. But it also showed that the strength of this relationship increased over time. In other words, economic forces and governmental policies had the effect of unintentionally transforming the self of the farmers and provoking collective resistance. When a relatively stable identity is threatened or disrupted—that is, endangered—it becomes more salient, group identification increases, and protest participation becomes more likely. In this way, the self serves as a critical social mechanism in the process of resisting inequality.

SUMMARY

In this chapter I have argued that the indignities and deprivations of inequality are never completely accepted as just or legitimate. We all need and desire the predictability and security of a stable social structure, but we are also motivated to live a life of dignity, respect, and equality. When the pain of exclusion and subservience becomes too much, we are compelled to resist and push back against the dominating structures of inequality. Resistance may be long-term and widespread, resulting in enduring changes for both self and society, or it may be small, narrow, and quickly extinguished by the powerful forces of the status quo. At both ends of this spectrum, however, the self operates as an intervening social mechanism linking inequality and acts of resistance. This is evident at three distinct levels of analysis where identity categories are used in different ways to signal opposition, build solidarity, and mobilize collective action.

At the level of culture, resistance occurs when oppressed people object to the negative cultural interpretations of an identity category and strive to create their own more positive and more powerful identity meanings. We see this, for example, in the case of gay rights where historically devalued categories of homosexual, lesbian, and queer have become more acceptable and less stigmatizing in the wider cultural arena. This transformation was facilitated by the development of social movement organizations and the emergence of a collective identity where gay people formed communities of solidarity and a commitment to collective action.

Resistance at the level of interaction occurs in settings where two or more people are engaged in face-to-face communication. In normal situations these everyday encounters proceed routinely and without disruption as participants follow expected rules of etiquette and good behavior. But this established interaction order often reflects and reinforces a taken-for-granted system of inequality where rituals of deference and demeanor privilege some identity categories over others. When a dominant interaction order is regularly disrupted by a series of public challenges, new identity meanings may emerge. We saw this, for example, in the US civil rights movement when rules of segregation and "racial etiquette" were intentionally violated, and when ordinary lunch counters, bus seats, and classrooms became sites of defiance and resistance.

Resistance at the person level is evident in the struggle for individual health and integrity. When social relationships and social institutions constrain access to valued identities, the self becomes susceptible to moral and physical injury, and when identity meanings bestow respect and dignity, the self is more likely to flourish and thrive. No single person has the power to transform an entire social system, but all acts of resistance do involve the self, and the most effective form of resistance at the person level happens when a collective identity is internalized. When this occurs, a strong personal commitment to resistance develops, group identification is enhanced, and a motivation to act accordingly becomes more compelling. Here it is important to recognize that the internalization of a collective identity is not exclusively psychological; it presupposes the existence of group solidarity, it depends upon supportive social ties, and it requires a degree of consistency with preexisting identities. This was evident, for example, among the college student civil rights activists who participated in the Freedom Summer Project. Their commitment to the campaign was reinforced by a collective identity that was in turn linked to other membership organizations, career choices, and educational goals.

By now it should be apparent that the three levels of analysis that I have used throughout this book (person, interaction, and culture) are not completely independent of each other. The distinctions have at times been magnified for analytical purposes, but in truth, identities and inequalities are formed, maintained, and altered through a complicated web of social and psychological processes that are difficult to disentangle. Nevertheless, in the next and final chapter, I will attempt to offer a more accurate (albeit complex) accounting of the relationship between the micro-dynamics of identity and the macrostructures of inequality.

5

WHAT IS THE RELATIONSHIP BETWEEN MICRO INEQUALITY AND MACRO INEQUALITY?

Up to this point I have addressed four fundamental questions about identity and inequality (chapters 1 through 4), and in answering them, my goal has been to review and integrate a diverse body of theory and research in a manner that is both academically sound and at the same time accessible to a more general public. The question I take up in this final chapter is more complex, more theoretically abstract, and less well understood.

Even though my emphasis in this book has been on the social self, interaction among persons, and the meaning of identity categories (micro-sociological processes), I have stressed throughout each of the first four chapters that inequality cannot be *reduced* to problems of identity. Identity processes are necessary for the making and breaking of inequality, but identity alone cannot explain the complex patterns of inequality that our species has created. Indeed, the operation of identity categories only makes sense if we take into account the larger sociological context within which identity categories and identity meanings develop, become entrenched, and are intentionally altered.

As I noted in chapter 1, inequality in human societies is much more than the simple competition among individuals for valued resources. Because our species has the capacity to communicate with symbols and engage in symbolic interaction, inequality for *Homo sapiens* is also associated with a wide range of cultural, economic, and political rules for allocating more resources to some people and less to others. In addition to creating identity categories for connecting individuals to differing amounts of value, power, and privilege, human inequality depends upon the creation and maintenance of powerful institutions where domination and exploitation is legitimated. For this reason, a complete understanding of inequality in human societies requires an examination of both micro-level social processes (interactions among persons) and macro-level social processes (patterns of social relationships).

Here I will address this issue more directly and provide a general overview of the relationship between micro- and macro-social processes. Because the discussion that follows is rather abstract, I have mapped out the major concepts and themes in figure 5.1. After explaining the relationship among the elements represented in the diagram, I will offer several empirical examples to help concretize the process.

THE EMERGENCE OF THE MACRO FROM THE MICRO

I live in the heart of Oregon's Willamette Valley, a majestic river drainage cutting through the verdant Pacific Coast Range and the rugged, snow-capped Cascade Mountains. It is a fertile agricultural basin sprinkled with small towns, row crops, hop fields, vineyards, and Christmas tree farms. As I type these words on an early spring morning I can hear the familiar honking of the Canada geese that spend their winters here before migrating north this time of year. If I were to peer out my office window at this moment, I would no doubt catch a glimpse of the overhead flock in their recognizable V formation.

For millennia, people have gazed upward in admiration of migrating geese and asked, "How do they organize their flight with such symmetry and structure?" Scientific evidence suggests that the V pattern is aeronautically efficient in that it allows each bird to draft off its neighbor in order to minimize drag and maximize lift. We also know that geese will rotate the leadership position so that no one bird is always doing the hardest work. Still, knowing that the V formation is functional for migration purposes does not tell us *how* the structure is created.

Over the years, many theories have been proposed to explain the coordinated behavior of bird flocks. Ancient Romans believed that flight patterns were a signal from the gods, and more recent accounts have hypothesized everything from "biological radio" and "natural telepathy" to the existence of a "group soul." The problem with these theories is that they assume that a regimented, recurring structure of individual positions in a group requires either simultaneous communication among all group members or the operation of some "higher power."

We now know that the explanation is much simpler. With the help of computer simulations and mathematical modeling, scientists have discovered that V formations (as well as other flock structures) are the *emergent* consequence of interaction between each individual bird and its nearest neighbor. As long as each member of the flock follows a few simple rules (e.g., find the channel of air with the least resistance), a coordinated group pattern will develop and be sustained even as a bird's nearest neighbor changes. In other words, group structure and group behavior can develop without a master plan, without a lead organizer, and without a system of communication that connects all members.

The geese that appear so elegant, regimented, and coordinated as they fly overhead do not "intend" to form a V structure, nor are they aware of the larger pattern that they display. The macro pattern of social relationships (the structure) so essential to the survival of their species is the consequence of a few micro-level interactions between each bird and its neighbor.[1]

I share this example of bird behavior because it illustrates two basic sociological principles that also apply to *human* interaction. First, micro-level, face-to-face interaction among persons will also produce regular patterns of social relationships that have a coordinated macro-level structure. Second, like birds, we are not always aware of the macrostructures that our micro-interactions produce. When each of us follows a few simple rules of interaction, we, too, unintentionally create larger patterns of social relationships that have real social consequences. We saw this, for example, in chapter 3, where I showed how macrosystems of status and power are often reproduced without intention or planning on our part.

But there is one very big difference between birds and *Homo sapiens*. Unlike persons, birds do not have the capacity for self-consciousness, they are incapable of planning, and no bird is able to intentionally create or alter social rules and patterns of social relationships. For this reason, the macro-level structures that emerge from human social interaction are not entirely equivalent to those found in a flock of birds, a school of fish, a beehive, or a wolf pack. The capacity for self-awareness that has evolved in our species has resulted in the ability to invent social identities, create cultural rules, and plan complex systems of power and privilege. And because these social constructions can be intentionally altered, the structures that emerge from our interactions are more pliable and less permanent than those found in other animal societies. Macro-level systems certainly have an effect on our behavior, and our micro-level interactions often give rise to larger social structures, but our distinctive capacity for agency makes the relationship between our micro and macro processes uniquely complex. I have outlined this dynamic process in figure 5.1.

The bottom half of the figure represents micro processes at the level of interaction. These are the everyday encounters we have with each other as we navigate our way through life. Much of this behavior is routine and does not require a great deal in the way of problem-solving, but because human behavior is premised on symbolic interaction, we

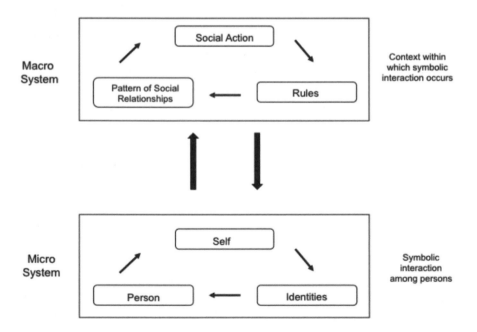

Figure 5.1.   The Interdependency of Micro- and Macrosystems

retain the capacity to adjust to novel situations or problematic encounters should they arise. This means that micro-level processes always have a degree of indeterminacy and unpredictability.

Inside the micro box are three concepts that were introduced in chapter 2. Each represents a different dimension of our individuality; when taken together, they form what we typically recognize as the qualities of a conscious, acting human being. Each of us enters this world as a *person* with a physical body subject to the laws of nature. The person is the location of our biological system and the hub of our subjective experience. The material and corporeal reality of persons is associated with the practical activities of physical survival—finding ways to eat, shelter, procreate, and avoid harm. When material resources necessary for survival are unavailable or are unevenly distributed, there are objectively negative consequences for the body and the mind.

The *self* refers to a set of dynamic social practices involving role-taking, self-reflection, and self-evaluation. Persons do not have these abilities when they are born. It is only through regular and intense social interaction that the self develops. In this sense, we can say that the self *emerges* from the person—but it is an emergence that presupposes a community of other persons communicating through symbolic interaction (especially language). Persons with the ability to take the perspective of others are more empathetic and are more likely to recognize when human dignity has been denied. This is a capacity that is highly evolved in our species, and it is a competence that is necessary if resistance to inequality is to be successfully organized.

Identities are the culturally recognizable categories that we use to name persons. All human societies employ identity categories, but at the same time, there is no such thing as a universal identity. Both the catalog of existing identities and the meanings associated with these identities will vary across groups, organizations, cultures, and historical time periods. This is because identities are social constructions (human inventions) that depend upon the self-processes of persons engaged in symbolic interaction. Because identities structure interaction, motivate behavior, influence our cognitions, and shape our emotions, they play a critical role in the making and breaking of inequality. And as the arrow connecting identities to persons suggests, identities are ultimately embodied. We cannot divorce personhood from identity categories, as they are the inevitable consequence of human interaction. Perhaps most critically, once identities emerge, they work back on persons by constraining and enabling the way we live, affecting, among other aspects, our relative wealth and status, our power and privilege, and our mental and physical health.

It should be obvious that the micro-level processes described in the bottom half of the diagram do not operate in a social vacuum. Similar to the flight patterns formed by flocks of birds, our micro-level interactions sustain enduring patterns of social relationships that define the context within which our symbolic interaction occurs.

The box at the top of the diagram represents the complex macrosystem that emerges from the lower-level micro processes. But notice also that there are two arrows connecting the micro and macro boxes. Interaction at the micro level gives rise to a macrosystem, and once established, the emergent macrosystem acts back on persons and situations. I will describe this process in more detail shortly, but first I will explain the relationship among the three elements included in the macro box.

As already noted, human interaction results in durable *patterns of social relationships*. These take many forms and can range from the simple structure of a family or sports team to the complex structure of a large governmental agency or multinational corporation. Some of these patterns are intentionally initiated, while others are the unintended outcome of rule-following behavior at the micro level (similar to that of geese). In the case of inequality, the patterns of most interest are those in which groups or classes of individuals are stratified in a hierarchy of wealth, income, status, power, and privilege. Residential segregation by race is one such pattern, as is the division of household labor by gender. One of the most consequential patterns of all is that between employees and managers, or workers and capitalists.

Established structures of social relationships both enable and constrain *social action*. When African Americans are in a dependent relationship with banks for real-estate loans, their housing options are constrained; when women are in a dependent relationship with men for income, their labor options are constrained; and when workers are in a dependent relationship with capitalists for jobs, their freedom to earn a living is also constrained. On the other hand, when groups are in a position of relative power, social action is enabled. Bankers can control who owns homes and in which neighborhoods. Men can limit the choices available to women, and capitalists can coerce workers to follow employment rules.

There is little doubt that *rules* govern social action. We can easily recognize the way in which legal statutes, social norms, religious doctrines, and employee handbooks influence our own individual behavior. But equally significant is the manner in which these same rules emerge from social action. Rules are dependent upon rule followers and rule enforcers—agents of social action. There could be a law that limits the speed of cars on interstate highways, but if not a single person obeys the law and no one ever enforces it, this particular law would exist only on paper. This is even more obvious in the case of "unwritten rules" such as those guiding etiquette, appropriate dress, or conversational turn-taking. We only recognize these rules when they are violated, and the evidence of rule violation is found in other people's objections and sanctions.

It should be clear that economic rules governing the distribution of resources are especially central to the establishment and reproduction of unequal social relations. For example, tax laws, minimum wage laws, the profit maximization rule, laws of inheritance, and rules that guide the labor market, all contribute to the relative degree of economic inequality in a society. Sociologist Douglas Porpora nicely captures this point when he articulates the distinction among rules, social relations, and action in a capitalist economy:

> Rules of allocation may make workers dependent on capitalists for jobs, but the dependency itself is neither a behavior nor a rule. There are no rules saying that workers are to depend on capitalists for their livelihood. Such dependency is a relationship. This relationship, to be sure, is a consequence of rules of allocation, but it is a consequence that itself has consequences. It enables the capitalist to coerce the worker into submitting to (among other things) the rules of authorization that obtain at the job site.[2]

Here it is important to emphasize that even though the macrosystem emerges from micro processes at the level of interaction, it also directly affects the microsystem by shaping identities and the material conditions necessary for persons to thrive. Put more abstractly, we can say that the micro and the macro are in a *dialectical relationship* of emergence and downward causation. Relationships of inequality emerge from self and identity processes, and these macro patterns of social relations both enable and constrain individual behavior. In the following section I will demonstrate the practical implications of this dynamic relationship with a concrete example borrowed from a study investigating identity, rules, and relationships in a large grocery store chain in which a union-organizing drive developed and was eventually quashed.

NEGOTIATING ORGANIZATIONAL CHANGE

Sometime in the late 1970s an ambitious young couple borrowed money from family and friends and opened a natural foods grocery store. Two years later, the determined, countercultural vegetarians merged their thriving business with another health-oriented grocery store in the same town. Success would follow. Over the next decade, the company opened new stores in different cities and states, and in the 1990s they began purchasing other natural food grocery chains. The company now operates 440 stores in the United States, Canada, and the United Kingdom and employs over ninety thousand people.

With their emphasis on organic food, the promotion of an environmental ethic, and a staff of young, socially conscious employees (many with visible piercings and tattoos), the company, early on, established a reputation as a hip, left-leaning, unconventional corporation with an employee-centered work culture. But as the company expanded, management practices began to change, and a significant number of employees grew frustrated with the transformation. So much so, that workers at several stores began agitating for union representation, initiating organizing drives in 2002. Corporate leadership, however, was not accommodating, and company executives mounted a vigorous campaign to extinguish the unions and banish labor activists. They were successful. As of April 2017, not a single store in the company chain has a union contract with its employees.

Why did the workers decide it was time to affiliate with a union? Why did the company fight back? What steps did the company take to control its employees? How were these social processes related to the growth of the company? These are some of the questions that sociologist Tricia McTague sought to answer in her case study of the Green Grocers store chain (a pseudonym used by McTague to protect the identity of the employees she interviewed). In this section I will review some of McTague's findings in an attempt to illustrate key features of the micro-macro relationship discussed above.[3] One especially valuable contribution of McTague's research is her consideration of *identity contests* as central to the relationship between an international corporation and its workers.

Identity Contests, Identity Rewards, and Identity Threats

The modern for-profit corporation is an example of a macrostructure of patterned social relations where organizational positions are associated with a clear hierarchy of power and status. It is also a place where formal and informal rules, policies, and practices are used to maximize earnings and control employee behavior. The organizational structure of the corporation is never static; if it is to survive in a competitive economic environment, it must adapt to various social and political mandates, develop novel products or services, adopt new technologies, and secure access to needed resources. In other words, as the surrounding sociological context changes, the corporation will need to change its structure and adjust its policies and practices as it develops creative strategies to ensure the maximization of profit.

But external, environmental forces are not the only sources of organizational change. Less obvious but equally significant are the internal dynamics and micro-level social processes that contribute to changes in organizational structure. We see this, for example, in the changing meanings, definitions, and expectations of the various work roles and managerial positions within a company—formally represented in changes to an organizational chart.[4] One of the most significant internal challenges for any business organization is the problem of employee recruitment and retention. High employee turnover and vacant organizational positions can threaten company success and make it difficult to adjust to external pressures. For this reason, organizations use rewards to induce compliance, sustain commitment, and maintain employee motivation. When the organization is a for-profit business, the financial rewards of employment become the primary motivation for employee loyalty—few of us would continue on the job if our employer suddenly stopped paying us. But money is not the only benefit or source of job satisfaction.

Organizations also use social and psychological rewards to elicit cooperation and encourage conformity. Recognition for a job well done, promotion to a position with more responsibility and status, or the granting of opportunities for creative expression are all desirable benefits that are likely to maintain employee motivation and assist in the recruitment of new workers. These inducements are rarely specified in employee handbooks or employment contracts, but they are rewards that often matter as much as one's wage. This is because the rewards that we care about the most are often those that are closely aligned with our identity categories.

Corporations are not simply profit-maximizing, economic machines. They are also places where significant social relationships and interpersonal friendship networks develop; as such, they contribute to the construction of personally salient identities. One is never just a worker or simply an employee; one might be an "aeronautical engineer working with a team on the design of a fuel system for the Boeing 787 Dreamliner at the Everett, Washington plant," or a "first year, third grade teacher working with twenty-three students in a bilingual classroom in room 220 at Englewood school in Salem, Oregon." In other words, our jobs situate us in very precise social and geographic locations. This is why being fired or laid off can be so devastating. In addition to losing an income, the unemployed are also stripped of a reliable identity; they are yanked from a network of dependable social relationships, and as a consequence, their usual sense of self is threatened.

For players of the game of capitalism there are social and psychological benefits associated with one's position in a corporation, and these can be understood as a type of *identity reward*.[5] When a company has an admirable public reputation, produces top-quality products, is highly selective in its hiring, or does work associated with intelligence and creativity, the identity rewards may be considerable. In these leading corporations, the self-regard of its employees will be enhanced and loyalty to the company will be strong. But if the company falters in some way—a financial scandal, charges of sexism, or corruption or bribery allegations—the value of its identity rewards will be diminished and employee motivation and commitment will likely decline. Sometimes a change in company policy can also affect identity rewards and negatively impact employee trust and satisfaction. This is what Tricia McTague discovered in her study of "Green Grocers" (GG).

As a grocery store chain, GG distinguishes itself with an intentional emphasis on environmental stewardship, healthy living, concern for local farms and "an unshakable commitment to sustainable agriculture." GG also advertises its commitment to "empowering work environments" where "motivated team members can flourish and succeed to their highest potential."[6] Any customer visiting GG for the first time would immediately notice a unique shopping atmosphere. There is an abundance of informational signage touting organic and locally grown products. Reusable shopping bags and recyclable materials are emphasized and encouraged. Handwritten chalkboard messages publicize the health benefits of specific herbs, and announce community meetings, cooking recipes, and yoga lessons. Stories and images of "local farmers" are displayed in aisles alongside bulk containers of products intended to reduce the reliance on packaging. It is a place where vegetarian, vegan, gluten-free, cage-free, free-range, and anti-GMO customers can shop with confidence, secure in the notion that their consumption needs and ecological-political values will not be compromised. Not surprisingly, it is also an atmosphere that has attracted young workers who share the same principles.

In interviews with employees at a store in the Midwest, McTague found that many young people sought jobs at GG because of the opportunity for self-expression and personal freedom. In contrast to other major chains where uniforms and conformity are mandated, GG workers could wear their own clothes, fashion unconventional hairstyles, show off tattoos and piercings, and even wear buttons and T shirts with political messages. "GG workers often said that they sought jobs at GG *because* they were environmentalists, vegans, foodies, sustainable-agriculture advocates, locavores, or health nuts."[7] In other words, the corporate culture was one that supported a range of "green identities" and the opportunity to reap certain identity rewards not readily available in most corporate workplaces. For this reason, many workers at the midwestern store studied by McTague experienced anger and disappointment when the company introduced policy changes and gradually began to redefine the store's public image. For these workers, changes to the company rules and practices were experienced as a threat to the valued meanings of a personally salient work identity.

Response to an *identity threat* can range from individual, psychological adjustments at the micro level, to collective action aimed at restoring or altering an organizational structure at the macro level. When a group of employees collectively resists a new policy or a change in identity rewards, we can say that an *identity contest* has emerged. In the case of GG, it was a contest between corporate managers on one side and store workers on the other. The corporate executives at GG initiated policy changes in an attempt to move the midwestern store away from the co-op/hippie vibe and toward a more mainstream image that would appeal to a wider and more upscale customer base. A more rigid dress code was introduced, piercings and bright hair color were forbidden, and buttons and T-shirts with political messages were no longer permitted. In addition, at about the same time, the expanding store chain negotiated supply deals with large agricultural producers and dropped contracts with many local farmers. For company executives, the shift meant greater profit and an increase in stock value. But for company workers, the shift was seen as a desertion of core values and was experienced as an assault on the self. This point was articulated well by one employee, a gender nonconformist who came close to quitting when the new dress policy was announced.

> I don't think I could ever make you understand just how much the dress code issue hurt me. I have spent my life trying to like, or at least not hate, myself because of all of the many ways in which I am considered socially unacceptable and the constant rejection I feel from the world around me. My guess is that no one reading this letter and certainly no one who created that dress code knows what it is like not to have a gender identity that is recognized by your culture. So in a place where this freaky little trannyboydyke [*sic*] found friends and found people who almost understood and people who accepted, there suddenly was the threat of losing my job, my means of supporting myself, because of my social unacceptability.[8]

Other workers with salient green identities objected to changes in policy that led to more waste and the discarding of unsold or expired products:

> But then all the product that was just past expiration or you know the product was fine but the packaging was damaged, we had to throw out and you know, for environmentally conscious people that was a really hard thing to be told we have to do. So that was another sort of—it felt very sort of hypocritical at that point.[9]

From the perspective of many workers, GG was denying them the opportunity to affirm their identities, a promised identity reward was being withheld, and the new corporate policies were viewed as a threat to established identity meanings. Moreover, because many employees experienced the same or similar identity threats, a collective response was provoked in the form of a union-organizing drive.

Returning once again to figure 5.1, we can see how new *rules* (in the macrostructure) were disturbing a normal *pattern of social relationships*, and this disruption initiated *social action* in an attempt to change the rules. The new organizational policies instituted by GG executives had the intended effect of changing the behavior (and fashion) of frontline service workers, but in disrupting the usual pattern of social relationships, unintended social actions were also instigated: a defensive response on the part of workers. Workers began to organize collectively in an attempt to change the rules of the organization and redefine the employer-employee relationship.

But this is only part of the story (the top half). We cannot fully understand the events at GG unless we also take into account the force of identity at the micro level as diagrammed in the bottom half of figure 5.1. Because of our capacity for *selfhood*, we experience ourselves as objects, we evaluate our actions from the point of view of others, and our self-regard largely reflects our assessment of others' evaluations of us. For this reason, we care about the shared meaning of our *identity* categories, and understand (at least implicitly) that one's dignity as a *person* is at stake when identity meanings are altered in an unfavorable way. The new company policies were so disruptive *because* they altered identity meanings, reduced identity rewards, and threatened self-regard.

Of course, union organizing is also provoked by the absolute and relative deprivation of financial rewards (a point that was made in chapter 4), and McTague offers evidence to suggest that low wages at GG also contributed to the frustrations of employees. But the power to control material rewards is only one part of the capitalist-worker relationship. Workers are also dependent on capitalists for identity rewards. According to figure 5.1, this coercive and unequal relationship emerges from symbolic interaction at the micro level, but once established, the downward causation of the macrostructures will limit the range of options and choices that are available to persons. We are free to act, but our action is constrained by the macro context.

Here it is important to emphasize that the interchange between the micro and the macro processes in figure 5.1 is not a closed system. The arrows that point from the bottom to the top and from the top to the bottom do not represent an impenetrable loop. Social forces outside of the immediate context of symbolic interaction are also influential. We see this, for example, in the case of the GG company executives who initiated changes to corporate policy in response to *external* market demands. And we see this also in the actions of GG employees who organized a drive to bring in union representation *external* to the company. The pattern of social relationships that defines the GG corporation is shaped in part by powerful managers who are motivated by the rules of capitalism to secure greater profit, and it is shaped in part by the less powerful workers who are motivated to secure greater material rewards, more control of policy decisions, and more respect and dignity. Both groups act to advance their interests and seek out tools and resources necessary to achieve their goals.

One of the more valuable resources for groups seeking greater equality is found in the power of identity itself. I have already described this in some detail in chapter 4, but in the following section I will introduce the idea of *identity transposition* as a particularly valuable strategy for changing durable patterns of social relationships from the ground up.

IDENTITY TRANSPOSITION AND STRUCTURAL CHANGE

A maximum-security prison is one of the most rigid and controlling institutions found in modern society. One need only examine the architectural structure of a prison building to appreciate the corporeal power and control it enables. Razor wire fences, immense concrete walls, iron bars, and security glass windows establish the physical context for everyday interactions. The unequal pattern of social relationships inside the prison walls is also visible and obvious. Uniforms distinguishing correctional officers from inmates mark formal positions, and the hierarchical authority structure among correctional staff is signaled with badges, stripes, and titles typically stitched onto the uniforms. It is difficult to imagine an institution where structural change is less likely to occur from the ground up.

Still, prison inmates do experience physical, social, and psychological deprivations that violate community standards of human dignity and reasonable care. And when unacceptable prison conditions persist, inmates will at times collectively organize in an effort to protect their health and defend their humanity. However, because inmates have few if any resources outside of their physical strength, a common form of protest is the so-called prison riot, which typically involves destruction of property and violent behavior. Even though inmates outnumber correctional staff, riots fail for obvious reasons: Correctional staff possess weapons, authorities can impose added punishment for rule-breakers, and the institution can draw additional personnel and material support from other governmental institutions.

An alternative to the prison riot is an organized, nonviolent form of protest where inmates refuse to cooperate with the regimented prison routine and ignore the commands of correctional officers. Such attempts to change prison conditions typically take the form of hunger strikes, work stoppages, or sit-ins. Although this type of collective action receives less publicity, it is nearly twice as common as the prison riot. In a survey of US prisons conducted in 1986, for example, researchers found that nearly 10 percent of prisons had experienced a riot in that year, but 18 percent reported a nonviolent protest involving ten or more inmates.[10] It is in these nonviolent protests that we find examples of *identity transposition*, as inmates draw upon new identities from outside of the institution to advocate for change.

Identity transposition occurs when a person borrows an identity from one structural location where it is commonly found and transports it to a different structural location where it is either uncommon or unwelcome.[11] Think, for example, of a gay activist who advertises his "deviant" sexual identity in a conservative religious assembly, a woman who enters an exclusive men's club, or an African American who intentionally breaches racial segregation laws. These deliberate violations of identity norms are meant to provoke social change by disrupting social relationships where power and privilege are firmly entrenched.

An example of how identity transposition works in a prison setting can be found in a study I conducted of an uprising by inmates at the Oregon Women's Correctional Center (OWCC). This "disturbance" occurred in 1988, when twenty-eight inmates gathered in a circle in the prison recreational yard and refused officer commands to return to their cells. The sit-down resistance was organized to protest living conditions within the prison. A small group of inmate leaders secretly planned the demonstration over several weeks. They identified a specific day and time for the event, instructed family and friends on the outside to notify the press in advance, and they prepared a four-page, handwritten declaration that listed fourteen "requests," including improved medical care, more sanitary showers, relief from overcrowding, and the reestablishment of education programs.

Two hours after the protest began, the "tactical emergency response team" from the neighboring men's prison entered the yard. Seven specially trained officers outfitted with helmets, batons, and shotguns marched slowly in a wedge formation toward the protesting inmates. When the women responded by linking arms, several officers moved, in coordinated fashion, to physically separate the demonstrators, systematically forcing their faces to the ground before cuffing their hands behind their backs. One by one, each inmate was then escorted back to the prison dayroom, where another team of correctional officers (both male and female) ordered the removal of all clothing for the purpose of conducting a full body "skin search."

The uprising was effectively extinguished within a matter of hours, and none of the inmate requests was met. The event received relatively little press coverage despite the fact that a newspaper reporter had arrived at the institution after receiving an anonymous tip. My own knowledge of the protest came several years later during a conversation with one of the inmates. [12]

There is nothing especially unique about this particular prison uprising, and one could certainly interpret it from a number of different sociological perspectives, but my intent here is to use it as an example of how identity can be used as a resource in the struggle for social change. As inmates, the women of OWCC had few options for collective action. Their physical confinement and control were the objectives of the staff and the sole purposes of the institution. Freedom of movement, personal discretion, and the public airing of grievances were not allowed. The women were objects of what sociologist Erving Goffman called a *total institution*, where established social relationships are purposely

cut off and a new, all-encompassing identity as inmate is forcibly im-
planted:

> The recruit comes into the institution with a self and with attach-
> ments to supports which had allowed this self to survive. Upon en-
> trance, he is immediately stripped of his wonted supports, and his
> self is systematically, if often unintentionally, mortified. . . . The
> stripping processes through which mortification of the self occurs are
> fairly standard in our total institutions. Personal identity equipment
> is removed, as well as other possessions with which the inmate may
> have identified himself, there typically being a system of nonaccess-
> ible storage from which the inmate can only reobtain his effects
> should he leave the institution. As a substitute for what has been
> taken away, institutional issue is provided, but this will be the same
> for large categories of inmates and will be regularly repossessed by
> the institution.[13]

But the debasement of the self in a total institution is never completely
successful. While prison walls might limit the importing of *physical
objects* and restrict contact with outsiders, a wall cannot contain the
circulation of *cultural objects* or eliminate contact among prisoners on
the inside. Inmates are usually free to interact with each other, and
these conversations often revive and support preferred identity catego
rics associated with more positive meanings. Sometimes interaction
among prisoners also leads to the discovery and adoption of new identities that have the potential to disrupt the structure of the institution.

This is what occurred at OWCC. When the women decided to agi-
tate for change *inside* the prison walls, they looked for identity resources *outside* the prison. What they found was a familiar cultural
script (*action schema*) associated with social protest. Although none of
the women protesters had any prior experience with political action,
community organizing, or public demonstrations, they were able to perform a coordinated nonviolent protest identity. Put another way, the
protester identity was *transposed* onto the institutional structure of the
prison.

We see this, for example, in the prepared statement that was de-
livered to prison officials. The first sentence of the document reads:
"Let it be known to Staff and Administration of Oregon Women's Correctional Center that on today's date October 1, 1988, a quiet, peaceful

sitdown demonstration has been called together by the Inmate Residents of Oregon Women's Correction Center." Here we see the women acknowledging their institutional identities ("inmate residents") while at the same time claiming new identities as nonviolent demonstrators. The last line of the declaration further clarifies the meaning of the new protest identity: "Let it also be known that there are inmates who have sworn to a Hunger Strike until these issues are met and resolved."

The inmate residents of OWCC also enacted their newly transposed identity with recognizable behaviors associated with nonviolent demonstrations. In addition to drafting a list of demands and staging a sit-in, the women also joined in singing the chorus to John Lennon's "Give Peace a Chance"—with a slight alteration of the original lyric ("All we are saying, is *let us be heard*"). Most inmates who did not take part in the sit-down provided supportive action by validating the protester identity with acts of solidarity. For a period of three hours following the "arrest" of the demonstrators, the inmate population filled the corridors of the prison with protest songs, shouts of anger, and the banging of hands and objects on the metal cell doors. And once the protesters were segregated from the general population they were collectively referred to as the "Twenty-Eight They Hate," a phrase that recalls similar characterizations of more famous groups of political prisoners such as the "Chicago Seven" and the "Gang of Four."

By transposing the protester identity into the normal operation of the prison, the women posed a threat to the established structure of the institution by violating its normal and expected pattern of social relationships. In fact, my own analysis of the uprising suggests that the peaceful protest at OWCC was more intimidating and more threatening to the structure of the prison than a violent riot. This is because correctional institutions are prepared to respond to violence, they train for riots, they expect violent confrontations, they wear armor and use weapons, and they employ a system of command and control that is modeled after militaristic organizations—but they are not organized to respond to peaceful resistance.

Indirect evidence of the power of the protest identity can be found in the harsh punishment that was levied against the twenty-eight women activists. Most of the protesters spent a full year in "segregation," and a small group of leaders spent over a year and a half in solitary confinement. This amount of "seg time" was highly unusual and was perceived by inmates as unreasonable and excessive. In contrast, a historical review of other disciplinary actions showed that inmates who had engaged in violent disturbances, such as fighting and rioting, received substantially less time in segregation. Indeed, the psychological consequences of the solitary confinement were so severe that two women had to be transferred to the Oregon State Hospital psychiatric ward.

One would think that acts of violence would be considered a more serious threat to the operation of the institution, but because the social structure of a prison is organized around violence, the transposition of a peaceful protest identity may actually be more disruptive. In the end, the protest did not alter prison life for the inmates largely because their actions did not successfully engage the wider public. The inmates themselves recognized that real change would not come from their "requests" but from political and public pressure on the outside. This is why they made sure that allies outside of the prison were poised to notify the press. The protesters were hoping to shine a light on their poor living conditions and generate public sympathy and concern.

But even when identity transposition is expertly performed, the structure of the prison is not likely to change. The physical and sociological barriers are simply too strong. We are more likely to find examples of "effective" identity transposition, where actors with multiple identities circulate through multiple structural locations with a greater degree of freedom, outside of *total institutions*.

Consider, for example, the contributions of the civil rights activists from the North who helped southern activists overcome barriers to radical collective action in the early 1960s. Sociologist Francesca Polletta's analysis of the movement found that "outsiders," especially the student organizers who moved into rural areas at great risk to their personal safety, provoked a sense of obligation on the part of local black residents and challenged local religious leaders to become more politically active. Southern blacks were the primary agents of social change, but students contributed to the success of the movement by transposing their white (northern) identities onto an established pattern of racial segregation. They did not bring with them financial resources or physical weapons, but they were able to disrupt a system of racial deference that was impeding more radical action. As Polletta notes, "Outsiders didn't empower a powerless group, or enlighten the falsely conscious, but they did undermine the structural relations within the group that channeled resistance in a conservative direction."[14]

SUMMARY

We are more likely to recognize inequality in society if we take a step back from our own personal situation and observe how valued resources are generally distributed within our local community, our nation, and our globe. When we do this, we find disturbing examples of concentrated wealth (e.g., the richest 1 percent has more wealth than the rest of the world combined), uneven and unfair wage and salary payments (e.g., in the United States, women earn on average 20 percent less than men for doing the same or similar job), systematic discrimination by law enforcement and the courts (e.g., African American men in the United States are six times more likely to be incarcerated as white men), as well as segregation and exclusion based on sexual orientation and sexual behavior (e.g., seventy-two countries have laws that criminalize homosexual activity, and ten of those countries impose the death penalty).

How do such patterns of inequality develop, how are they sustained, and how do they change? Most sociologists will argue that macro-level patterns of inequality demand an equally *macro*-level sociological explanation. For this reason, sociologists look to institutional structures, historical events, political ideologies, and economic rules for explanations of inequality. What is it about capitalism, labor markets, political institutions, schools, and neighborhoods that helps produce and sustain inequality? This is a necessary approach, and these are important questions that should not be ignored.

In this book, however, I have departed from this more common "top-down" strategy by examining the problem of inequality in society from a *micro*-sociological perspective, which is to say from the "bottom up." Here my focus has been on the way in which various categories of identity are implicated in the making and breaking of power and privilege in society. My analysis does not dispute or contradict top-down explanations. In fact, I have stressed throughout this book that identity alone cannot explain the persistence of inequality or the transformation of society toward a more egalitarian distribution of valued resources. Indeed, in this final chapter I have attempted to show how the micro-social processes associated with identity are inextricably linked to the larger, macro patterns of social relations.

One particularly significant contribution of a sociological perspective is that it can demonstrate how actions of individual persons may unintentionally form larger social structures or patterns of social relations. Like migrating geese that unintentionally fly in a regimented V pattern, we are not always aware of the macro-level consequences of our micro-level actions. For this reason, it is easy to believe that as individuals we have no role in the production of inequality. It is tempting to assert, for example, that some people have more wealth simply because they work hard, possess more talent, or are blessed with superior skills. Or that people are poor because they lack a work ethic, are irresponsible, or were born without much talent. But in fact, structures of inequality are the collective consequence of our individual interactions with each other. In other words, the macro patterns of inequality that structure the distribution of wealth, power, and privilege in our society emerge from the micro processes of everyday life.

The macro system is at once the product of symbolic interaction among persons and the context within which the interaction occurs— that is, there is a dialectical relationship between the micro- and macro systems. Structures of inequality emerge from interaction among persons; once established, these same structures act back on actors, limiting opportunities for some while enabling opportunities for others. This is not an easy idea to comprehend, and the complexity of the interdependency between the micro processes and the emergent macrosystem can make our understanding of inequality difficult.

We can get a glimpse of this complex dialectical process at work if we examine how our personal identity categories work to both constrain and enable our own behavior. For example, most of us strive to achieve positive, respected, and rewarding identities while defending against being classified under categories that are perceived to be negative, worthless, or of little value. We prefer to think that who we are as persons is determined by our words and deeds, by how we treat others, by our personal accomplishments, and by our unique character. But this is never completely the case. The generalized cultural meanings attached to identity categories also matter, and these meanings are not under any single individual's control. Thus, you might be an honest, hardworking, gentle, and caring US citizen, but if you are a follower of

Islam you will struggle to gain respect, dignity, and acceptance in a society where nearly half of all adult Americans say they have an unfavorable attitude toward Muslims.[15] An identity category that elicits favorable evaluations is an asset; one that is viewed in negative terms can hinder one's ability to thrive.

In a society stratified by wealth and status, those with power often determine the rewards attached to an identity. We saw this, for example, in the case of the Green Grocers employees, many of whom saw a rewarding employee identity transformed by a more powerful employer. Top-level managers changed the rules of the workplace and, in "rebranding" the company, forced employees to change their behavior and alter their presentation of self, or risk losing employment. But changing how we act and dress and changing the culture of the company that we work for also changes the meaning of our own identity.

We need identity categories. It is impossible to live a normal social life as a fully functioning human without using identity categories. Identities are not simply words; they serve as the means for self-awareness, self-knowledge, and social interaction. We cannot on our own choose to ignore identity without suffering negative social consequences. Others assume that we will present ourselves through culturally acceptable identities. If we violate this assumption, others will do identity for us. This is because identity functions as a necessary sociological compass, providing orientation and direction in an otherwise bewildering social environment. Without mutually recognizable identity categories and identity meanings, we would be lost, unmoored, floating unpredictably in a sea of capricious and unknowable strangers.

While this book has emphasized how identity serves to legitimate and reproduce systems of inequality, I have also argued that identity is fundamental to the production of group solidarity and the organization of positive social change. As part of the macrosystem, identity categories may constrain our action, but as part of the microsystem, identities also serve as resources that enable behavior not otherwise possible. This is especially true for collective acts of resistance where identities can offer an outline for how to organize and protest in support of human dignity.

Even in the most repressive institutional settings, such as a maximum-security prison, a concentration camp, or a slave colony, we find examples of persons pushing back, challenging authority, revising identity scripts, creating new identity meanings, and breaking the downward causation of an oppressive macrosystem. We saw this illustrated in the example of women prisoners described earlier in this chapter. Under conditions of a *total institution*, where the self is intentionally mortified and stripped of individuality, and where action is controlled, monitored, and regimented on a daily basis, the motivation to resist and defend one's dignity remains. Absent material resources to fight back against institutionalized oppression, the women of OWCC collectively refused to accept the demands of the prisoner identity. In a united act of defiance, they imported and adopted the role of protester. They did not have to invent this category; in very general terms it was already familiar to them because it "existed" as an identity in their cultural toolbox. Even though the women prisoners had no prior experience as political activists or protest organizers, they were able to use the protest identity as a resource in their struggle for dignity.

Identity categories may be a universal and necessary feature of human social life, but specific identity meanings are not permanent; that is, the power and privilege attached to an identity category is not immutable. The same identity processes that sustain and reproduce systems of inequality may also be used to challenge and disrupt oppressive identity meanings and domineering identity practices. We know from history that egalitarian collective identities have emerged in support of resistance, reform, and revolution under some of the most tyrannical social conditions. Therefore hope is forever on the horizon, and as long as an ember of human dignity still glows, it is possible to stoke the fire of equality and justice. Even though the social forces of oppression and domination are enormously powerful, and the experience of being unequal may feel like destiny, resisting inequality is always at some level a collective option.

NOTES

INTRODUCTION

1. Thomas Piketty, *Capital in the Twenty-First Century* (Cambridge, MA: Harvard University Press, 2014), 571.

2. For an intellectual history of identity, see R. Martin and J. Barresi, *The Rise and Fall of Soul and Self: An Intellectual History of Personal Identity* (New York: Columbia University Press, 2013); C. Taylor, *Sources of the Self: The Making of the Modern Identity* (Cambridge, MA: Harvard University Press, 1989).

3. Psychological approaches to identity are represented in the following: E. H. Erikson, *Identity and the Life Cycle: Selected Papers* (New York: International Universities Press, 1959); M. R. Leary and J. P. Tangney, eds., *Handbook of Self and Identity* (New York: Guilford Press, 2011); N. Ellemers, R. Spears, and B. Doosje, "Self and Social Identity," *Annual Review of Psychology* 53, no. 1 (2002): 161–86; T. R. Tyler, R. M. Kramer, and O. P. John, *The Psychology of the Social Self* (New York: Psychology Press, 2014); S. J. Schwartz, K. Luyckx, and V. L. Vignoles, eds., *Handbook of Identity Theory and Research* (New York: Springer, 2011).

4. For a sampling of different sociological approaches to identity, see P. L. Callero, "The Sociology of the Self," *Annual Review of Sociology* 29 (2003): 115–33; J. A. Howard, "Social Psychology of Identities," *Annual Review of Sociology* 26 (2000): 367–93; R. Jenkins, *Social Identity* (New York: Routledge, 2014); H. Ferguson, *Self-Identity and Everyday Life* (New York: Routledge, 2009); S. Scott, *Negotiating Identity: Symbolic Interactionist Approaches to Social Identity* (Cambridge, UK: Polity, 2015); S. Lawler, *Identity: Sociological Perspectives* (Cambridge, UK: Polity Press, 2008); G. J. McCall and J. L. Sim-

mons, *Identities and Interactions* (New York: Free Press, 1966); P. J. Burke and J. E. Stets, *Identity Theory* (New York: Oxford University Press, 2009); C. Smith, *What Is a Person? Rethinking Humanity, Social Life, and the Moral Good from the Person Up* (Chicago: University of Chicago Press, 2010); M. Castells, *The Information Age: Economy, Society, and Culture*, vol. 2, *The Power of Identity*, 2nd ed. (Malden, MA: John Wiley and Sons, 2010); C. J. Calhoun, *Social Theory and the Politics of Identity* (Cambridge, MA: Blackwell, 1994); S. Stryker, T. J. Owens, and R. W. White, eds., *Self, Identity, and Social Movements*, vol. 13 (Minneapolis: University of Minnesota Press, 2000); A. Giddens, *Modernity and Self-Identity: Self and Society in the Late Modern Age* (Stanford, CA: Stanford University Press, 1991).

5. Many other US cities have similar streets, highways, and railroads that serve as boundary lines of racial segregation. For example, in Kansas City it is Troost Avenue, in Saint Louis it is Delmar Boulevard, and in Detroit it is Eight Mile Road. For maps of other cities and links to related resources, see Emily Badger and Darla Cameron, "How Railroads, Highways and Other Man-Made Lines Racially Divide America's Cities," *Washington Post*, Wonkblog, July 16, 2015, https://www.washingtonpost.com/news/wonk/wp/2015/07/16/how-railroads-highways-and-other-man-made-lines-racially-divide-americas-cities.

6. Catherine Silva, "Racial Restrictive Covenants: Enforcing Neighborhood Segregation in Seattle," Seattle Civil Rights and Labor History Project, http://depts.washington.edu/civilr/covenants_report.htm.

I. WHAT IS INEQUALITY?

1. Jane Goodall, *In the Shadow of Man* (New York: Houghton Mifflin Harcourt, 2000), 113.

2. Ibid., 114.

3. R. D. Fernald, "Communication about Social Status," *Current Opinion in Neurobiology* 28 (2014): 1–4.

4. See, for example, B. M. Knauft, "Violence and Sociality in Human Evolution," *Current Anthropology* 32, no. 4 (1991): 391–428; M. Dyble, G. D. Salali, N. Chaudhary, A. Page, D. Smith, J. Thompson, L. Vinicius, R. Mace, and A. B. Migliano, "Sex Equality Can Explain the Unique Social Structure of Hunter-Gatherer Bands," *Science* 348, no. 6236 (2015): 796–98.

5. J.-J. Rousseau, *Discourse on the Origin of Inequality* (New York: Oxford University Press, 2000).

6. C. Boehm, *Hierarchy in the Forest: The Evolution of Egalitarian Behavior* (Cambridge, MA: Harvard University Press, 1999).

7. Primatologist Frans de Waal offers compelling evidence that animal cognition is more complex and sophisticated than we have assumed. See his *Are We Smart Enough to Know How Smart Animals Are?* (New York: W. W. Norton, 2016). In the past, comparing the minds of humans and other animals has led to a ranking of species that has blinded researchers and created an unnecessary hierarchy of intelligence. My emphasis on difference in certain capacities is not intended to suggest superiority in all types of intelligence.

8. There is less agreement over the identification and operation of the different levels of analysis. Nevertheless, a conceptual distinction offered by E. O. Wright is consistent with the general position taken in this book. According to Wright, there are three clusters of causal mechanisms: (1) *individual attributes and life conditions* linked to the acquisition of valuable resources; (2) *opportunity hoarding*, where boundaries and economic advantages are linked to social positions; and (3) *exploitation and domination* tied to power relations among positions. See Wright's chapter, "Logics of Class Analysis," in *Social Class: How Does It Work?* ed. A. Lareau and D. Conley (New York: Russell Sage Foundation, 2008), 329–49.

9. See Nick Estes, "Border Town, USA: An Ugly Reality Many Natives Call Home," Indian Country Media Network, August 15, 2014, http:// indiancountrytodaymedianetwork.com/2014/08/15/border-town-usa-ugly-reality-many-natives-call-home-156414.

10. For a comprehensive anthology of different sociological approaches to inequality, see D. B. Grusky, *Social Stratification*, 4th ed. (Boulder: Westview, 2014).

11. Quoted by Nick Estes in "Welcome to Gallup, NM, where 'They Just Want Another Person Dead,'" Indian Country Media Network, August 29, 2014, https://indiancountrymedianetwork.com/news/politics/welcome-to-gallup-nm-where-they-just-want-another-person-dead.

2. WHAT DOES IDENTITY HAVE TO DO WITH INEQUALITY?

1. The following quotes are from B. Lucal, "What It Means to Be Gendered Me: Life on the Boundaries of a Dichotomous Gender System," *Gender and Society* 13, no. 6 (1999): 781–97. For an influential explanation of gender as an interactional accomplishment see C. West and D. H. Zimmerman, "Doing Gender," *Gender and Society* 1, no. 2 (1987): 125–51.

2. J. Henson, *Father Henson's Story of His Own Life*, No. 1796 (Boston: JP Jewett and Cleveland: HPB Jewett, 1858).

3. W. J. Anderson, *Life and Narrative of William J. Anderson, Twenty-Four Years a Slave* (Daily Tribune Book and Job Printing Office, 1857).

4. H. A. Jacobs, *Incidents in the Life of a Slave Girl: Written by Herself*, ed. L. Maria Child (Boston: Published for the Author, 1861).

5. For an excellent psychological analysis of dehumanization, see D. L. Smith, *Less Than Human: Why We Demean, Enslave, and Exterminate Others* (New York: St. Martin's Press, 2011).

6. T. Jefferson, *The Papers of Thomas Jefferson*, Retirement series, vol. 7 (Princeton, NJ: Princeton University Press, 2010).

7. A. Hitler, *Mein Kampf* (Uttar Pradesh, India: Om Books International, 2010).

8. R. J. Sharpe and P. I. McMahon, *The Persons' Case: The Origins and Legacy of the Fight for Legal Personhood* (Toronto: University of Toronto Press, 2008).

9. This is also why both opponents and defenders of legal abortion argue for the protection of human dignity. For opponents, the fetus is considered a defenseless person in need of protection from the state. Defenders of abortion rights argue that the dignity of the mother is at risk and deserves protection. For an example of how human dignity has been employed in legal arguments for and against abortion, see R. Dixon and M. C. Nussbaum, "Abortion, Dignity and a Capabilities Approach" (Public Law Working Paper 345, University of Chicago, 2011).

10. H. J. Paton, *The Categorical Imperative: A Study in Kant's Moral Philosophy*, vol. 1023 (Philadelphia: University of Pennsylvania Press, 1971).

11. C. Smith, *What Is a Person? Rethinking Humanity, Social Life, and the Moral Good from the Person Up* (Chicago: University of Chicago Press, 2010), 435–36.

12. See J. R. Simmons Jr., *Factory Lives: Four Nineteenth-Century Working-Class Autobiographies* (Peterborough, Canada: Broadview Press, 2007). This passage is from "A Memoir of Robert Blincoe," written by journalist John Brown in 1828.

13. Ron Sauder, "Emory Declares Its Regret for Historic Involvement with Slavery," January 17, 2011, http://www.emory.edu/EMORY_REPORT/stories/2011/01/campus_regret_for_historic_involvement_with_slavery.html.

14. D. Blankenhorn, "How My View on Gay Marriage Changed," *New York Times*, June 22, 2012.

15. G. H. Mead, *Mind, Self and Society* (Chicago: University of Chicago Press, 1934), 7–8.

16. "Statement of Regret," Emory University, http://www.emoryhistory.emory.edu/issues/challenges/discrimination/slavery/regret.html.

17. D. Keltner and R. J. Robinson, "Defending the Status Quo: Power and Bias in Social Conflict," *Personality and Social Psychology Bulletin* 23, no. 10 (1997): 1066–77; N. Eisenberg, B. C. Murphy, and S. Shepard, "The Develop-

ment of Empathic Accuracy," in *Empathic Accuracy*, ed. W. Ickes (New York: Guilford Press, 1997): 73–116.

18. S. T. Fiske, "Controlling Other People: The Impact of Power on Stereotyping," *American Psychologist* 48, no. 6 (1993): 621.

19. T. P. Love and J. L. Davis, "The Effect of Status on Role-Taking Accuracy," *American Sociological Review* 79, no. 59 (2014): 848–65.

20. A. G. Gitter, H. Black, and D. Mostofsky, "Race and Sex in the Communication of Emotion," *Journal of Social Psychology* 88, no. 2 (1972): 273–76; J. M. Howells and P. Brosnan, "The Ability to Predict Workers' Preferences: A Research Exercise," *Human Relations* 25, no. 3 (1972): 265–81; S. Wheeler, "Socialization in Correctional Communities," *American Sociological Review* 26 (1961): 697–712.

21. P. Perry, *Shades of White: White Kids and Racial Identities in High School* (Durham, NC: Duke University Press, 2002).

22. Ibid., 35.

23. Ibid., 49.

24. Ibid., 50.

25. Ibid., 82.

26. J. Bettie, *Women without Class: Girls, Race, and Identity* (Berkeley: University of California Press, 2014).

27. Ibid., 17.

28. M. Lamont, *The Dignity of Working Men* (New York: Russell Sage Foundation, 2000).

29. Ibid., 64.

30. Ibid., 79.

31. Lucal, "What It Means to Be Gendered Me."

32. W. B. Swann Jr., "The Self and Identity Negotiation," *Interaction Studies* 6, no. 1 (2005): 69–83.

33. Q. D. Atkinson, "Phonemic Diversity Supports a Serial Founder Effect Model of Language Expansion from Africa," *Science* 332, no. 6027 (2011): 346–49.

34. For an elaboration of this process, see C. Tilly, *Identities, Boundaries, and Social Ties* (Boulder, CO: Paradigm Publishers, 2005).

35. A. C. Wilkins, "Becoming Black Women: Intimate Stories and Intersectional Identities," *Social Psychology Quarterly* 75, no. 2 (2012): 173–96.

36. Ibid., 181.

37. Ibid.

38. Ibid., 183.

39. Ibid., 189.

40. C. A. Sue, *Land of the Cosmic Race: Race Mixture, Racism, and Blackness in Mexico* (New York: Oxford University Press, 2013), 31.

41. Ibid., 41.

42. C. E. Osgood, G. J. Suci, and P. H. Tannenbaum, *The Measurement of Meaning* (Urbana: University of Illinois Press, 1978).

43. H. C. Triandis, *Analysis of Subjective Culture* (New York: Wiley-Interscience, 1972); H. C. Triandis, *Individualism and Collectivism* (Boulder, CO: Westview Press, 1995).

44. T. D. Kemper and R. Collins, "Dimensions of Microinteraction," *American Journal of Sociology* 96 (1990): 32–68.

45. S. B. Westley and M. K. Choe, "How Does Son Preference Affect Populations in Asia?" (Asia Pacific Issues Working Paper 84, East-West Center, Honolulu, 2007).

46. E. W. Kane, "'No Way My Boys Are Going to Be Like That!' Parents' Responses to Children's Gender Nonconformity," *Gender and Society* 20, no. 2 (2006): 149–76.

47. Ibid., 167–68.

48. For related findings, see T. Langford and N. J. MacKinnon, "The Affective Bases for the Gendering of Traits: Comparing the United States and Canada," *Social Psychology Quarterly* 35 (2000): 34–48. Here it is important to note that the level of culture represents a rather abstract collective that can vary in size, shared history, common ancestry, regional similarity, religious tradition, and other social commonalities. In some instances, cultural boundaries may be coterminous with group boundaries. See G. A. Fine, *Tiny Publics: A Theory of Group Action and Culture* (New York: Russell Sage Foundation, 2012).

49. J. R. Feagin and D. Van Ausdale, *The First R: How Children Learn Race and Racism* (Lanham, MD: Rowman & Littlefield, 2001).

50. T. Stivers and A. Majid, "Questioning Children: Interactional Evidence of Implicit Bias in Medical Interviews," *Social Psychology Quarterly* 70, no. 4 (2007): 424–41.

51. R. Harlow, "'Race Doesn't Matter, but . . .': The Effect of Race on Professors' Experiences and Emotion Management in the Undergraduate College Classroom," *Social Psychology Quarterly* 66 (2003): 348–63. See also A. Aguirre Jr., *Women and Minority Faculty in the Academic Workplace: Recruitment, Retention, and Academic Culture*, ASHE-ERIC Higher Education Report, vol. 27, no. 6 (San Francisco: Jossey-Bass, 2000); T. Chambers, J. Lewis, and P. Kerezsi, "African American Faculty and White American Students Cross-Cultural Pedagogy in Counselor Preparation Programs," *Counseling Psychologist* 23, no. 1 (1995): 43–62.

52. Harlow, "Race Doesn't Matter, but . . . ," 354.

53. Ibid., 352.

54. A. R. Hochschild, *The Managed Heart: Commercialization of Human Feeling* (Berkeley: University of California Press, 2003).

55. J. Aronson, M. J. Lustina, C. Good, K. Keough, C. M. Steele, and J. Brown, "When White Men Can't Do Math: Necessary and Sufficient Factors in Stereotype Threat," *Journal of Experimental Social Psychology* 35 (1999): 29–46.

56. S. J. Spencer, C. M. Steele, and D. M. Quinn, "Stereotype Threat and Women's Math Performance," *Journal of Experimental Social Psychology* 35, no. 1 (1999): 4–28.

57. J. Stone, C. I. Lynch, M. Sjomeling, and J. M. Darley, "Stereotype Threat Effects on Black and White Athletic Performance," *Journal of Personality and Social Psychology* 77, no. 6 (1999): 1213.

58. J. M. Silva, *Coming Up Short: Working-Class Adulthood in an Age of Uncertainty* (New York: Oxford University Press, 2013).

59. Ibid., 29.

60. The relationship between social inequality and health inequality is multifaceted and complex, involving factors at multiple levels of analysis. For an excellent summary and analysis of this literature, see J. D. McLeod, "Social Stratification and Inequality," in *Handbook of the Sociology of Mental Health* (New York: Springer, 2013), 229–53; J. D. McLeod, C. Erving, and J. Caputo, "Health Inequalities," in *Handbook of the Social Psychology of Inequality*, eds. J. McLeod, E. Lawler, and M. Schwalbe (New York: Springer, 2014), 715–42.

61. R. Sennett, and J. Cobb, *The Hidden Injuries of Class* (New York: Vintage, 1972).

62. Ibid., 30.

3. HOW DOES IDENTITY CONTRIBUTE TO THE REPRODUCTION OF INEQUALITY?

1. US Bureau of Labor Statistics, "Highlights of Women's Earnings in 2012," *BLS Reports*, Report 1045, October 2013, https://www.bls.gov/opub/reports/womens-earnings/archive/womensearnings_2012.pdf.

2. Rakesh Kochhar and Richard Fry, "Wealth Inequality Has Widened along Racial, Ethnic Lines since End of Great Recession," Pew Research Center Fact Tank, December 12, 2014, http://www.pewresearch.org/fact-tank/2014/12/12/racial-wealth-gaps-great-recession.

3. For an extensive analysis of the growth in African American incarceration rates, see M. Alexander, *The New Jim Crow: Mass Incarceration in the Age of Colorblindness* (New York: New Press, 2012).

4. My analysis is limited to how identity processes contribute to the reproduction of inequality. For a more inclusive interactionist analysis of reproduction, see the excellent work of Michael Schwalbe and his colleagues, especially

M. Schwalbe, D. Holden, D. Schrock, S. Godwin, S. Thompson, and M. Wol-komir, "Generic Processes in the Reproduction of Inequality: An Interactionist Analysis," *Social Forces* 79, no. 2 (2000): 419–52.

5. M. O. Hunt, "African American, Hispanic, and White Beliefs about Black/White Inequality, 1977–2004," *American Sociological Review* 72, no. 3 (2007), 390–415; J. R. Kluegel and E. R. Smith, *Beliefs about Inequality: Americans' Views of What Is and What Ought to Be* (New York: A. de Gruyter, 1986).

6. See B. Gates, "Why Inequality Matters," Gates Notes, October 13, 2014, http://www.gatesnotes.com/Books/Why-Inequality-Matters-Capital-in-21st-Century-Review.

7. Joleen Kirschenman and Kathryn M. Neckerman, "'We'd Love to Hire Them, but . . .' : The Meaning of Race for Employers," in *The Urban Under-class*, ed. C. Jencks and P. E. Peterson (Washington, DC: Brookings Institu-tion, 1991), 203–32.

8. Ibid., 221.

9. Ibid., 209.

10. Ibid., 223–24.

11. P. Bourdieu, *Outline of a Theory of Practice* (Cambridge: Cambridge University Press, 1977); P. Bourdieu, *Distinction: A Social Critique of the Judgement of Taste* (Cambridge, MA: Harvard University Press, 1984); P. Bourdieu, "The Forms of Capital," in *Handbook of Theory and Research for the Sociology of Education*, ed. J. G. Richardson (New York: Greenwood Press, 1986), 241–58.

12. M. Bertrand and S. Mullainathan, "Are Emily and Greg More Employ-able than Lakisha and Jamal? A Field Experiment on Labor Market Discrimi-nation," *American Economic Review* 94, no. 4 (2004): 991–1013.

13. D. Pager and B. Western, "Identifying Discrimination at Work: The Use of Field Experiments," *Journal of Social Issues* 68, no. 2 (2012): 221–37.

14. C. A. Moss-Racusin, J. F. Dovidio, V. L. Brescoll, M. J. Graham, and J. Handelsman, "Science Faculty's Subtle Gender Biases Favor Male Students," *Proceedings of the National Academy of Sciences* 109, no. 41 (2012): 16474–79; W. A. Darity and P. L. Mason, "Evidence on Discrimination in Employment: Codes of Color, Codes of Gender," *Journal of Economic Perspectives* 12, no. 2 (1998): 63–90.

15. D. Neumar, R. J. Bank, and K. D. Van Nort, "Sex Discrimination in Restaurant Hiring: An Audit Study" (National Bureau of Economic Research Working Paper w5024, Washington, DC, 1995).

16. C. Goldin and C. Rouse, "Orchestrating Impartiality: The Impact of "Blind" Auditions on Female Musicians" (National Bureau of Economic Re-search Working Paper w5903, Washington, DC, 1997).

17. For a more detailed analysis of discrimination in job ads, see Darity and Mason, "Evidence on Discrimination."

18. O. Alonso-Villar, C. Del Rio, and C. Gradín, "The Extent of Occupational Segregation in the United States: Differences by Race, Ethnicity, and Gender," *Industrial Relations: A Journal of Economy and Society* 51, no. 2 (2012): 179–212.

19. P. N. Cohen and M. L. Huffman, "Occupational Segregation and the Devaluation of Women's Work across US Labor Markets," *Social Forces* 81, no. 3 (2003): 881–908; L. Catanzarite, "Brown-Collar Jobs: Occupational Segregation and Earnings of Recent-Immigrant Latinos," *Sociological Perspectives* 43, no. 1 (2000): 45–75; B. Ehrenreich and A. R. Hochschild, *Global Woman: Nannies, Maids, and Sex Workers in the New Economy* (New York: Macmillan, 2003).

20. L. Burnham and N. Theodore, *Home Economics: The Invisible and Unregulated World of Domestic Work* (New York: National Domestic Workers Alliance, 2012).

21. One reason that domestic labor was considered undignified was that it was often associated with sexual abuse. Young women working in private homes were often in vulnerable, unsafe positions with little recourse if they were assaulted.

22. H. R. Diner, *Erin's Daughters in America: Irish Immigrant Women in the Nineteenth Century* (Baltimore: Johns Hopkins University Press, 1983), 82.

23. For a more in-depth analysis of domestic labor, see M. Romero, *Maid in the USA* (New York: Routledge, 1992); P. Hondagneu-Sotelo, *Domestica: Immigrant Workers Cleaning and Caring in the Shadows of Affluence* (Berkeley: University of California Press, 2007); D. M. Katzman, *Seven Days a Week: Women and Domestic Service in Industrializing America* (Urbana: University of Illinois Press, 1981).

24. Katzman, *Seven Days a Week*, 188.

25. Hondagneu-Sotelo, *Domestica*, 31.

26. Romero, *Maid in the USA*, 144.

27. Hondagneu-Sotelo, *Domestica*, 217.

28. E. Goffman, *Interaction Ritual: Essays on Face-to-Face Interaction* (New York: Pantheon Books, 1967), 57.

29. Ibid., 58.

30. The phrase is usually attributed to Eleanor Roosevelt. See E. Roosevelt, *This Is My Story* (Boston: Houghton Mifflin, 1965).

31. Schwalbe et al., "Generic Processes in the Reproduction of Inequality."

32. C. L. Ridgeway, *Framed by Gender: How Gender Inequality Persists in the Modern World* (New York: Oxford University Press, 2011), 7.

33. For a more detailed examination of cognitive structures, person perception, and identity stereotypes, see D. J. Schneider, *The Psychology of Stereotyping* (New York: Guilford Press, 2005).

34. R. E. Petty, R. H. Fazio, and P. Briñol, eds., *Attitudes: Insights from the New Implicit Measures* (New York: Psychology Press, 2012).

35. J. F. Dovidio and S. L. Gaertner, "Aversive Racism and Selection Decisions: 1989 and 1999," *Psychological Science* 11, no. 4 (2000): 315–19.

36. D. R. Heise, *Expressive Order: Confirming Sentiments in Social Actions* (New York: Springer Science and Business Media, 2007).

37. J. Rollins, *Between Women: Domestics and Their Employers* (Philadelphia: Temple University Press, 1987), 162.

38. For a comprehensive review of affect control theory, computer simulations, and mathematical models, see Heise, *Expressive Order*. For a more recent review of affect control theory and its relevance to inequality, see S. Foy, R. Freeland, A. Miles, K. B. Rogers, and L. Smith-Lovin, "Emotions and Affect as Source, Outcome and Resistance to Inequality," in *Handbook of the Social Psychology of Inequality*, ed. J. D. McLeod, E. J. Lawler, and M. Schwalbe (New York: Springer, 2014), 295–324.

39. A. D. Cast, J. E. Stets, and P. J. Burke, "Does the Self Conform to the Views of Others?" *Social Psychology Quarterly* 62 (1999): 68–82.

4. HOW IS IDENTITY USED TO RESIST INEQUALITY?

1. A. Shaw and K. R. Olson, "Children Discard a Resource to Avoid Inequity," *Journal of Experimental Psychology: General* 141, no. 2 (2012): 382.

2. K. McAuliffe, P. R. Blake, G. Kim, R. W. Wrangham, and F. Warneken, "Social Influences on Inequity Aversion in Children," *PLOS ONE* 8, no. 12 (2013): e80966.

3. T. Malti, M. Gummerum, S. Ongley, M. Chaparro, M. Nola, and N. Y. Bae, "'Who Is Worthy of My Generosity?' Recipient Characteristics and the Development of Children's Sharing," *International Journal of Behavioral Development* 40, no. 1 (2016): 31–40.

4. R. Wilkinson and K. Pickett, "The Importance of the Labour Movement in Reducing Inequality," Center for Labour and Social Studies, July 2014, http://classonline.org.uk/docs/2013_04_Thinkpiece_-_labour_movement_and_a_more_equal_society.pdf.

5. M. Kleykamp and J. Rosenfeld, "How the Decline of Unions Has Increased Racial Inequality," *Arguments: A Blog from the Editors and Writers of*

Democracy, August 30, 2013, http://www.democracyjournal.org/arguments/ 2013/08/how-the-decline-of-unions-has-increased-racial-inequality.php.

6. B. Western and J. Rosenfeld, "Unions, Norms, and the Rise in US Wage Inequality," *American Sociological Review* 76, no. 4 (2011): 513–37.

7. E. Fischer, *The Good Life: Aspiration, Dignity, and the Anthropology of Wellbeing* (Stanford, CA: Stanford University Press, 2014), 17.

8. R. Fantasia, *Cultures of Solidarity: Consciousness, Action, and Contemporary American Workers* (Berkeley: University of California Press, 1989).

9. Ibid., 92.

10. T. W. Smith and J. Son, *Trends in Public Attitudes about Sexual Morality* (Chicago: NORC at the University of Chicago, 2013).

11. J. D'Emilio, "Capitalism and Gay Identity," reprinted in *The Gender/ Sexuality Reader*, ed. R. N. Lancaster and M. di Leonardo (New York: Routledge, 1997), 169–78.

This is not a unique assertion; related evidence regarding the historical emergence of the homosexual identity has been famously offered by M. Foucault, *The History of Sexuality*, vol. 1, *An Introduction*, trans. Robert Hurley (New York: Pantheon, 1978).

12. Today, of course, we recognize many more identity categories under the banner of gay identity. The abbreviation LGBT continues to expand as more specific types of sexual identities are recognized and legitimated.

13. "About Us," Human Rights Campaign, http://www.hrc.org/the-hrc-story/about-us.

14. J. Gamson, *Freaks Talk Back: Tabloid Talk Shows and Sexual Nonconformity* (Chicago: University of Chicago Press, 1998).

15. For sociological analyses of culture wars, see J. D. Hunter, *Culture Wars: The Struggle to Define America* (New York: Basic Books, 1992); T. Gitlin, *The Twilight of Common Dreams: Why America Is Wracked by Culture Wars* (New York: Metropolitan Books, 1995); M. Parenti, *The Culture Struggle* (New York: Seven Stories Press, 2011).

16. E. Goffman, "The Interaction Order: American Sociological Association, 1982 Presidential Address," *American Sociological Review* 48, no. 1 (1983): 1–17.

17. J. C. Scott, *Domination and the Arts of Resistance: Hidden Transcripts* (New Haven, CT: Yale University Press, 1990), 136.

18. R. Hodson, *Dignity at Work* (Cambridge, UK: Cambridge University Press, 2001).

19. For representative studies of schools, see P. E. Willis, *Learning to Labor: How Working Class Kids Get Working Class Jobs* (New York: Columbia University Press, 1977); J. MacLeod, *Ain't No Makin' It: Leveled Aspirations in a Low-Income Neighborhood* (1987; Boulder, CO: Westview, 1995), e-book.

For representative studies of neighborhoods, see E. Anderson, *Code of the Street: Decency, Violence, and the Moral Life of the Inner City* (New York: W. W. Norton, 2000); D. J. Harding, *Living the Drama: Community, Conflict, and Culture among Inner-City Boys* (Chicago: University of Chicago Press, 2010).

20. A. Pollert, *Girls, Wives, Factory Lives* (London: Macmillan, 1981), 152–53.

21. L. J. Alston and J. P. Ferrie, "Paternalism in Agricultural Labor Contracts in the US South: Implications for the Growth of the Welfare State," *American Economic Review* 83, no. 4 (1993): 852–76.

22. J. W. Harris, "Etiquette, Lynching, and Racial Boundaries in Southern History: A Mississippi Example," *American Historical Review* 100, no. 2 (1995): 387–410.

23. For a more general examination of symbolic codes of purity within cultural systems, see M. Douglas, *Purity and Danger: An Analysis of Concepts of Pollution and Taboo* (London: Routledge, 2003).

24. R. E. Park, "The Bases of Race Prejudice," *Annals of the American Academy of Political and Social Science* 140 (1928): 11–20.

A similar conclusion was reached in 1937 by Bertram Wilbur Doyle, an African American sociologist who assessed the role of racial etiquette in maintaining social control: "To the extent, then, that both agree upon this, we may say that the sentiments of both white and colored people support the mores and social ritual. Tradition thus assigns the Negro his status in the South, law defines it, sentiments support it, custom and habit continue it, and prejudice maintains it in those instances where it seems to be breaking down." See B. W. Doyle, *The Etiquette of Race Relations in the South* (Chicago: University of Chicago Press, 1937), 157.

25. A. Moody, *Coming of Age in Mississippi* (New York: Delta, 1968), 266.

26. A. Honneth, *Disrespect: The Normative Foundations of Critical Theory* (Cambridge, UK: Polity Press, 2007).

27. Anderson, *Code of the Street*, 33.

28. Ibid., 33–34.

29. According to Zoe Berko: "(T)he New York Police Department estimates that about 40 percent of the city's shootings involve members of violent crews of 12 to 20 year olds with most of this gun violence driven by incidents of disrespect." See Zoe A. Berko, "Street Code Adherence, Callous-Unemotional Traits and the Capacity of Violent Offending versus Non-Offending Urban Youth to Mentalize about Disrespect Murder," *CUNY Academic Works*, 2015, http://academicworks.cuny.edu/gc_etds/523.

30. Anderson, *Code of the Street*, 76.

31. For a more general sociological analysis of identity salience, see P. L. Callero, "Role-Identity Salience," *Social Psychology Quarterly* 48, no. 3

(1985): 203–15; S. Stryker and R. T. Serpe, "Identity Salience and Psychological Centrality: Equivalent, Overlapping, or Complementary Concepts?" *Social Psychology Quarterly* 57, no. 1 (1994): 16–35.

32. D. McAdam and R. Paulsen, "Specifying the Relationship between Social Ties and Activism," *American Journal of Sociology* 99, no. 3 (1993): 640–67.

33. Ibid., 662.

34. B. Klandermans and M. de Weerd, "Group Identification and Political Protest," in *Self, Identity, and Social Movements*, ed. S. Stryker, T. J. Owens, and R. W. White (Minneapolis: University of Minnesota Press, 2000), 68–92.

5. WHAT IS THE RELATIONSHIP BETWEEN MICRO INEQUALITY AND MACRO INEQUALITY?

1. For an example, see T. Vicsek, A. Czirok, E. Ben Jacob, I. Cohen, and O. Schochet, "Novel Type of Phase Transitions in a System of Self Driven Particles," *Physical Review Letters* 75 (1995): 1226–29; C. Reynolds, "Flocks, Birds, and Schools: A Distributed Behavioral Model," *Computer Graphics* 21 (1987): 25–34.

2. D. V. Porpora, "Cultural Rules and Material Relations," *Sociological Theory* 11 (1993): 220.

3. I draw upon both McTague's doctoral dissertation research as well as additional analyses published in collaboration with her colleagues. See T. McTague, "Cultivating Consent, Reaping Resistance: Identity-Based Control and Unionization at a High-End Natural Foods Company" (PhD diss., North Carolina State University, 2010), https://repository.lib.ncsu.edu/handle/1840.16/6467; M. Schwalbe, T. McTague, and K. Parrotta, "Identity Contests and the Negotiation of Organizational Change," *Advances in Group Processes* 33 (2016): 57–92.

4. More generally, sociologist Michael Schwalbe reminds us that the "structure of capitalism" also depends on identity categories. "Identity is fundamental in the game of capitalism. Identity determines which moves a person can legitimately make. A person identified as the CEO of a corporation can hire and fire people, allocate resources, make company policy; a person identified as a secretary cannot. A person identified as the owner of a house can make the move of selling that house; a person identified as a passerby on the street cannot. A person identified as the rightful heir to a fortune can claim that fortune; a person with no known connection to the wealthy decedent cannot. Every kind of consequential move in the economic realm, or in the game of capitalism broadly construed, depends for its acceptability on the prior

establishment of identity." See M. Schwalbe, "The Astructural Bias Charge: Myth or Reality?" *Studies in Symbolic Interaction* 46 (2016): 95–122, esp. 101.

5. Schwalbe, McTague, and Parrotta, "Identity Contests."

6. Quotes are from the "Green Grocers" company website.

7. Schwalbe, McTague, and Parrotta, "Identity Contests," 77.

8. McTague, "Cultivating Consent," 105.

9. Ibid., 101.

10. B. Useem and M. D. Reisig, "Collective Action in Prisons: Protests, Disturbances, and Riots," *Criminology* 37, no. 4 (1999): 735–59.

11. The idea of identity transposition is similar to the more familiar concept of *schema transposition* elaborated by W. H. Sewell Jr., "A Theory of Structure: Duality, Agency, and Transformation," *American Journal of Sociology* 98, no. 1 (1992): 1–29.

12. At the time, I was doing some volunteer teaching inside the prison, and several of the protest leaders agreed to share with me their interpretation of the uprising. These conversations also lead to contacts with inmates who had subsequently been released. In addition, I received permission to copy official reports and documents archived by the institution.

13. Erving Goffman, "On the Characteristics of Total Institutions," in *Symposium on Preventive and Social Psychiatry* (Washington, DC: Walter Reed Army Medical Center, 1957), 43–84, esp. 49–50.

14. F. Polletta, "'Free Spaces' in Collective Action," *Theory and Society* 28 (1999): 1–38.

15. Shibley Telhami, "American Attitudes toward Muslims and Islam," Brookings Institution, July 2016, https://www.brookings.edu/research/american-attitudes-toward-muslims-and-islam.

INDEX

ABOUT THE AUTHOR

Peter L. Callero is professor of sociology at Western Oregon University. His research examines the self-society relationship and addresses questions concerning identity, altruism, and inequality. His other books are *The Myth of Individualism: How Social Forces Shape Our Lives*, *Giving Blood: The Development of an Altruistic Identity* (coauthored with Jane Piliavin), and *The Self-Society Dynamic: Cognition, Emotion, and Acti on* (coedited with Judith Howard).